Finding Company Sponsors

for Good Causes

DIRECTORY OF SOCIAL CHANGE

Finding Company Sponsors for Good Causes
Chris Wells

Published by
The Directory of Social Change
24 Stephenson Way
London NW1 2DP
Tel: 020 7209 5151; fax: 020 7209 5049
e-mail: info@dsc.org.uk
from whom further copies and a full publications list are available.

Copyright © The Directory of Social Change 2000

ISBN 1 900360 37 3

British Library Cataloguing in Publication Data
A catalogue record for this book is available from the British Library

Cover design by Linda Parker
Designed and typeset by Linda Parker
Printed and bound by Antony Rowe, Chippenham

Other Directory of Social Change departments in London:
Courses and Conferences tel: 020 7209 4949
Charity Centre tel: 020 7209 1015
Research and Marketing tel: 020 7209 4422
Finance tel: 020 7209 0902

Directory of Social Change Northern Office:
Federation House, Hope Street, Liverpool L1 9BW
Courses and Conferences tel: 0151 708 0117
Research tel: 0151 708 0136

Contents

Dedication

This book is dedicated to Mary Wells 1912–1998 who taught, by example, how to give and not to count the cost.

About the author

Chris Wells is a training consultant who conducts around 100 seminar and training days each year, across the length and breadth of the country, working with both the voluntary and commercial sectors. He is an energetic and enthusiastic course leader, whose delegates frequently comment on the motivating and inspiring elements of their training experience. Chris has worked with many household names to improve their marketing, communication, and management strategies. Author of the acclaimed *DIY Guide to Charity Newsletters*, when not training, Chris still finds time to be a churchwarden, School Governor and charity trustee ... not to mention his wife Grace and their 11 (eleven!) children.

Acknowledgements

Directory of Social Change would like to particularly thank British Heart Foundation, Save the Children and ACTIONAID for giving us permission to reproduce extracts from their brochures for the appendix.

Introduction

Do we really need another book about corporate fundraising?

Probably not. But then this isn't just another book about corporate fundraising. It is an attempt to look seriously at entry into one of the fastest growing and most lucrative sections of the corporate marketplace.

There was a time – it seems hard to remember now – when sponsorships and product placements were relatively rare and discreet. Today, the hurried, harassed, and ethical consumer is drowned in strap lines, branded links, and social marketing initiatives. The 1990s was the decade when sponsorship became an essential item in the marketing mix of the image-conscious company. The type and number of opportunities have increased sharply and swiftly, so that an activity which was initially limited to sport and the arts has extended to broadcasting, the community, and both national and local government. Mintel, a leading consumer market research company, estimates that the value of community support from companies grew 114% between 1992 and 1997.

Amidst all this frenetic activity, many smaller charities are being left behind: without the resources to buy in marketing expertise from the private sector; without the marketing budgets to attract corporate attention; and often without a real understanding of how very different this marketplace can be from traditional sources of funds. Charities have waded into this new trough of money, snouts to the fore, eyes firmly shut and they have often trodden right in the mire as a result!

There are constant complaints about fickle decisions, ethical nightmares, crushing disappointments following raised expectations, and constant misunderstandings. Corporate attitudes versus charity values brings about a clash of cultures that is neither surprising nor is it necessary. All that is needed is a bit of forethought, which is what this book is trying to help you develop. Forethought based, in the main, on the experiences of those brave souls who marched into this market first. The risks along with the headaches and errors were great, but as with any exploitation of early opportunity, so were the rewards.

In the competitive fundraising environment in which we live, it was the rewards that attracted attention. The size of the cheques that were being written made the daily round and common task of traditional fundraising look very hard work.

To be blunt, for some of you, reading this book will save you considerable pain, time and effort, as you will decide that sponsorship fundraising is not for you or your organisation. The first and most vital consideration for each of you is to understand that sponsorship requires the wholehearted support of your entire organisation. Delivering a sponsorship package reaches parts of your charity that other fundraising doesn't reach. This is both a pain and a huge boon. It is a pain because there genuinely are people who work in the voluntary sector because they prefer the values and approaches to life that are commonly held. As their wholehearted support is a prerequisite of a sponsorship deal, their rejection of commercial values and priorities can lead to real conflict within your organisation. The boon comes because through a process of explanation and debate – a winning of hearts and minds in support of a sponsorship package – you can energise and inspire your whole organisation. Enthusiasm and positive outlook can often result in benefits for both the commercial and voluntary sector sides of a charity partnership.

I've been training voluntary sector groups in how to find sponsors for more than a decade. When I began, I was quite gentle in the ways I explained to delegates why they, and/or their organisation, weren't ready for sponsorship. As any group of course attenders would tell you, now I'm pretty brutal. This is not an area for the faint-hearted; not a panacea for other fundraising failures; and not a substitute for shrinking local authority grants. You have to want to make this succeed; to want to work in a commercially aware manner; to want to change and be ever more businesslike in your operations; and to want the relationships with businesses, not just the money.

This book grew out of those training courses; when handouts and copies of OHP slides never seemed enough to answer all the questions and keep people moving forward. Of course, during those sessions one heard many examples of good and bad practice.

Sadly, mistakes and errors are more common, and educationally more helpful, than perfection. So a very big thank you to all those brave souls who allowed me to feature their stories in these pages. I've called them 'sagas' because often they were long and painful lessons for those involved. You get the benefit of the summary as a warning.

Other thank yous start with Grace, whose patience and fortitude underpins all that I do; Anne Mountfield, Alison Baxter and Bethany Rawles at the Directory of Social Change; and the British Heart Foundation, Save the Children Fund, and ACTIONAID for use of brochures as examples. If each and every one of you who reads this book can find one avenue to achieve new funds, it will have been more than worthwhile.

1 Donors and sponsors

· ·

- What's the difference between a donation and sponsorship?
- Who do we approach in the company?
- What do companies want from the deal?
- Why do companies reject our proposals?

The word 'sponsorship' is widely used, but is often no more than a thinly veiled demand for a donation to support a favoured cause. Companies and individuals are often assailed to sponsor walkers, silences, bike rides, dance competitions and so on, in aid of a particular charity. What is consistent about these approaches is that they offer no benefit to the donor, other than the warm healthy glow of doing good. This book is not about soliciting donations, but about commercial sponsorship, where the relationship between companies and fundraisers will be more involved, with greater and longer-lasting benefits to both parties.

The key element in commercial sponsorship is 'mutual benefit'. This is what many traditional fundraisers fail to understand when they go looking for corporate cash. Usually, when you organise a 'wine and wisdom' evening or a race night for your local school or church, you either get sponsors by approaching businesses that you know, or tap the donations budget of bigger businesses you don't know. If they know you, you'll get the money because you're a friend or a valued customer. With the bigger business you'll succeed because they want to be seen as a good citizen in the local community.

Real sponsorship fundraising must have much bigger and more tangible benefits than that. All of the examples quoted so far are 'one-offs' – a single event, a specific walk or activity, but that is not what this book is about. You can use the ideas and approaches to win money for one offs, but that is not my aim. The aim of this guide is to equip every reader with the chance to develop sponsorship fundraising as an ongoing source of income. Alongside events, trusts, and individual donations, sponsorship can become a vital part of your fundraising strategy. Some of you will have already had some success raising money from companies, others will understand how hard trying to get money from companies can be. Wherever you start, the important point to understand right now is that raising general donations from companies is very different from sponsorship fundraising.

Who to approach for a donation

Traditionally fundraisers have competed in the donations marketplace. Many companies set aside some money each year to be given to charitable activity. When, as a fundraiser, you talk to companies, initially the response tends to be that you should either contact their donations manager or that they're not a big enough company to have a donations budget. To some extent this may be true as it is usually only the larger corporations that have formal budgets. They tend to be listed in publications such as *The Guide to UK Company Giving* (see Resources) with contact names and guidelines for the type of activity supported. Where there is no formal budget, fundraisers often search for someone in the company with authority enough to divert some funding in their direction.

Even for larger companies the donations budget is not very big in commercial terms, and is almost always over-subscribed. Most commonly it is run as a paper-bound application process. You write to the relevant individual, having first checked that your cause fits the company guidelines. Sometimes you may get to meet, but that is much less common. Put yourself in that person's place and see it from their side. Think of who they are. Sometimes it's a company secretary, sometimes a community affairs manager, an employee fundraising committee representative, the managing director's PA, or a manager moved sideways to see out their time with the company.

These people enjoy a few characteristics in common that you must understand. They are not, and certainly this part of their activity is not, at the cutting edge of commercial concern. And like all people trusted with giving away somebody else's money, they have an almost exaggerated sense of care and some common fears. It is worth bearing the following in mind.

- They are afraid you'll turn out to be not the worthy organisation you say you are, but something dodgy that will put them on the front page of the newspapers tomorrow. As a result they ask you for masses of information – project outlines, budgets, accounts, annual reports etc. You have to assemble weighty amounts of paper in order to apply.
- Donations budgets are often under pressure. It is often habit to justify current budget levels by proving more could have been spent. If the person responsible can report the expenditure with a rider that another 5–10 times as much could have been spent on equally worthy causes, then they have a strong case for maintaining the budget at the same or a higher level next year.
- The process of applying for a donation can become a fairly crude 'beauty contest', where the charity that best fulfills the emotional tear-jerking criteria will gain support.
- Increasingly, companies expect and require the involvement of a company staff member with the charity to provide a recommendation/introduction.
- Decisions tend to be made each year, about the current year's budget.

I have often described this whole process as being a bit like achieving conviction under criminal law – you have to prove beyond reasonable doubt, with a high standard of written evidence that you are the best charity for them to support. Although this is an exaggeration, for most fundraisers companies are usually potentially more lucrative than they turn out to be, and can be quite hard work for any amount raised.

Who to approach for sponsorship

There is another budget that is infinitely bigger called the marketing/advertising budget. This budget is for you if you are looking for commercial sponsorship rather that a one-off donation. This is generally where sponsorship monies are sought and won. It is run very differently from the donations budget and with a very different view of life. The tactics for approach and success in the two areas are as different as chalk and cheese.

Firstly, as a fundraiser you have to understand that this budget is the lifeblood of the company. If it spends this money wisely and well, it will successfully sell its product or service, make profits and prosper (or at least survive). A warm healthy glow approach cuts no ice here. Instead, the staff in the marketing department are thinking of how your proposal will help inform, educate or sell in their company's marketplace.

Secondly, your competition for this budget are some of the sharpest and most effective sales teams in the country. TV, radio and magazine advertising is a multi-million pound industry, very serious about its revenue.

Thirdly, this budget is run, generally, by people with current commercial acumen, with both the company's profits and their careers in mind. Senior marketing people move jobs frequently to director level, a bigger plc, or a wider brief. They are always working to make an impact both in the company and for their CV.

As a result the right proposal will win support and a decision rather more quickly than under most donations budgets. It's a bit like working with the civil law: if, on the balance of evidence, you can convince the company that there is some benefit in it for them, the decision will swing your way. But you have to get access to the marketing department first.

Most companies almost automatically divert charities to the donations department. You have to get over this hurdle and achieve a face-to-face meeting with the people who count – paper alone will not work here; you have to convince them you're a credible potential *commercial* partner who can deliver your side of the bargain; you have to talk the language of target audience, reach, impact, and image if you're going to convince them.

What are sponsors looking for?

Most companies like sponsorship for straightforward reasons. Some of the factors that influence them are listed below.

Image

Sponsorship can create, enhance, or renew the image of a company. A company can sponsor an activity that works on that image. Being a good citizen may mean children's activities, community festivals, disabled access. Being an exciting organisation may mean hot-air balloon racing, slalom sports teams – anything fast and furious.

Sponsorship offers extra opportunities for public relations and advertising activity. Even something as simple as advertising on a litter bin can be enhanced by adding 'sponsored by' – indicating community involvement and good citizenship.

Sporting and gala events create greater promotional opportunities than conventional marketing approaches. Sponsorship scores over straight advertising as more subtle and less intrusive. Additionally, with the type of activity comes an image about the sponsor through the media. Think about which works better – paid advertising or personal recommendation? Personal recommendation is usually felt to be more truthful, and media coverage of sponsored activity is similar. It is editorial, which is seen as more honest, and therefore has a stronger impact on image.

Target

Sponsorship allows both audience and/or particular geographical area to be targeted accurately. It is vital that you understand quite clearly who you reach with your events and activities, and how that equates with the company's potential customers. Drug companies will sponsor medical charities which reach medical researchers and doctors; makers of green wellies like ecological groups; ethical investment companies appreciate the values of animal rights campaigners. If the target audience process works well, both direct marketing and sales promotions opportunities may open up for the company.

Media exposure

One of the main reasons why companies sponsor is to exploit public relations opportunities. Using PR approaches to get company names and views into the media is an established part of most companies' communications strategies. It is important to realise that sponsorship deals are about promoting corporate branding as much as anything else.

Look in any newspaper or at any television schedule and you will see events and activities linked to company names. The linkage with the good name of the sport or charity provides much added value to money being spent in parallel on advertising. In addition, many potential customers will watch or read who would not previously have thought of buying from this particular company. After seeing the link with their favourite sport or cause, now they just might try the product or service.

Prestige

If you, as a charity, have the appropriate event or image, then the style and class of the activity can rub off on the company sponsoring you. A Royal Gala says something about the company's image. Such events also allow customers to be entertained and impressed by the company's largesse and style.

Good corporate citizen

There is a growing awareness and concern for this particular reputation-builder. The CBI held its first conference on this issue on October 1997 'From the Board to the Brand'. Corporate citizenship is wider than just community relations – it involves being a good employer and providing a valued and useful product, as a way to promote external brand, image and reputation. According to Ben Leadsom, Head of Community Affairs at Barclays plc, it is 'a unique opportunity to enhance Barclays' corporate brand, reputation, image and health … [for] … the long-term welfare of the company'.

Cheap

The impact of a successful sponsorship is usually more cost effective than trying to achieve the same impact by other techniques. The named exposure in the media of a sponsor can often be bought for the cost of a minor advertising campaign.

Charities, in general, sell these benefits too cheaply – usually just amazed anyone will back their schemes at all!

Personal quirk

Never underestimate the impact of the personal interests of the decision maker. We're used to the idea of getting donations for a cancer charity from a family touched by the disease; corporate decision makers have their quirks and interests as well. They could be opera buffs, racing car enthusiasts, or could have a son or daughter tangled with drugs, happy memories of a scout troop … the list is endless. At other times they just get caught up in the excitement of the event.

> ● **SPONSORSHIP SAGA**
>
> There was a man who sought sponsors for rowing the Atlantic in a type of metal barrel. The daredevil received £500 from one sponsor for the first attempt – they also backed the second and third attempts spending more and more money. When on the fourth try he made it, only the sponsor joined the man's long-suffering wife to greet his arrival in Newfoundland. Having backed the adventure with more than £11,000 over the years, the sponsor was equally excited the rower had finally done it!

Why companies say 'no'

Most companies of any size are flooded with sponsorship proposals from charities – one large company PR manager talks in terms of 50+ every week. Most fail for the simplest reason of all: they are strong on what the charity wants, vague and weak on what the sponsor will get. This is the main reason companies say no, and why most of these proposals simply waste their time. Additional common reasons for an automatic 'no' are listed below.

Wrong image or target audience

When we write to a company we often research them and their marketplace, but most companies publish what they have been doing, not what they intend to do – for fairly obvious reasons linked to the competitive nature of the marketplace. We want to sell them the benefits of matching their target audience and image with ours, but often guess what their future targets may be. That's the value and necessity of meeting them face to face, as it is only then that we can ask the right questions and get that fundamental objective right.

Value

The sponsorship package is not seen by the company as good value, or it is too expensive or too late for this year's budget. Sponsorship is also notoriously difficult to measure. Evaluating success is a vital area for negotiation.

Donation

There is so little visible 'mutual benefit' in the proposal, or the company doesn't realise this charity is taking a different approach, that the proposal is viewed in donation terms. One common fear here is that sponsoring/donating to one high-profile activity will lead to hundreds more proposals from fundraisers. It is sadly true. As soon as they see a company sponsoring something, fundraisers feel that somebody else has already done the hard bit – selling the concept – and the company must be willing to try it again with a different cause.

Scope and control

Sponsorship often involves many different departments – PR, sales, advertising, marketing, sales promotion etc. For all of these to contribute and liaise with one another demands considerable time and effort from executives and managers, even before possible entertaining and attendance commitments. If staff resources will be over-stretched, they may be reluctant to get involved.

Personal quirk (again!)

You can have a perfectly-targeted proposal, to the right decision maker at the correct time – yet somehow it just doesn't have the spark that comes from personal interest to make it work. The decision maker in the company may understand how perfectly well this matches the company's needs, but they may be affected by personal beliefs or prejudices. If individually they believe the homeless are in part responsible for their own condition, or disabled facilities are the responsibility of government, or famines are about political decisions not lack of resources, this is bound to influence the final decision. However, remember that the personal spark can also tip the balance in your favour, helping to overcome some of their other worries.

NOW DECIDE:
- *Are you aiming for a one-off donation or long-term sponsorship?*
- *Can you compete in the commercial marketplace?*
- *Can you talk the language of reach, impact and image?*
- *What does your organisation have to offer companies?*

---

2 The sponsor's view

- What sort of company structures are there?
- What does CRM really mean?
- How long does all this take?
- Where does this fit with other company marketing objectives?

National or local company?

When you are going to approach a company for sponsorship there are some obvious questions to ask yourself. Outside the top charities, most voluntary organisations have a local or regional bias and therefore a company with a local presence will almost certainly be where you begin. Generally there are three types of local presence:

- Local branch office of a national company.
- Head office of a national company.
- Local or regional company.

Each of these will have a different view of the image your sponsorship may create, the target area it will reach, and the target audience that will be available. For example, a national company promoting a new product or service will probably want national reach, whilst a local company battling with the council for planning permission will be happy strengthening community ties. Similarly many local companies will not have marketing departments or PR advisers, and may need some persuading that sponsorship is a cost-effective form of advertising for them, whereas the national company may have developed sophisticated marketing strategies whose goals are beyond the means of any other than genuinely national charities.

Cause-related marketing

At the top end of decision–making you'll probably encounter quite complex views of what a sponsorship may achieve. The American concept of 'corporate responsibility' underlies these views, but even more critical is the notion of cause-related marketing.

Cause-related marketing (CRM) is one of the big growth areas in budgetary expenditure, and as big company players become more multinational than purely national, developments in marketing thinking globally have their effects. American Express is usually credited with bringing CRM into real public view with its 1983 campaign to raise funds for the restoration of the Statue of Liberty. It offered a $10 donation for each new card issued and a smaller contribution for each transaction billed to the card. The overwhelming public response raised $5m. By 1992 the CRM market in North America was worth $250m, and has more than doubled in value again since then.

In part of Dominic Cadbury's (Chairman of Cadbury Schweppes) report to shareholders, at the Annual General Meeting in 1997, he stresses the importance of CRM.

'Before looking ahead, I wanted to draw your attention to our continued focus on community support in areas where we can bring relevant experience and resources in addition to financial support. In particular, I would like to highlight the leadership we have provided in conjunction with Business in the Community to the development of cause-related marketing which links companies' promotional programmes with charitable causes for mutual benefit. In this way marketing activities and investment can benefit directly the needs of the community.'

CRM research

Companies like sponsorship and CRM principles because it gives them a return on their expenditure; charities because it unlocks newer, larger, budgets. Do the public like these ideas? In 1994 in North America the Cone/Roper Benchmark Survey on cause-related marketing underscores that they do:

- **78%** of adults said they'd be more likely to buy a product associated with a cause they care about.

- **66%** of adults said they'd switch brands.
- **62%** said they'd switch retailers to support a cause.
- **54%** claimed they would pay more for a product to support a cause they cared for.

Interestingly, the greatest impact was amongst the group classed as 'influentials'. This consists of people who have attended college and have higher than average incomes. They also, as a group, were much more likely to be able to name a company that has used unacceptable marketing practices.

At the time of writing, Mintel had just published some UK research, entitled Cause-Related Marketing. Although the research is less sophisticated and developed than the Cone/Roper Benchmark survey, it demonstrated similar public views.

- **77%** of interviewees would be likely to buy a product that supported a good cause.
- **50%** claimed they were willing to change brands.
- **60%** appear willing to pay more for a cause-related product, with strong support from women, younger consumers, and oddly, benefit dependants.

The figures Mintel have reported are remarkably consistent with the US finding. However, they must be balanced against some of the alternative responses from the Mintel research.

- **70%** of consumers believe social responsibility lies with government.
- **60%** of consumers claimed to have never taken part in a CRM activity or were unsure.
- **60%** of consumers agree that 'companies are just cashing in on public sympathy to increase sales'.

Mintel concludes that the lack of awareness about the good causes that businesses support provides companies and marketing strategists with opportunities. CRM appears to be developing a momentum of its own, with more enlightened and aware consumers coming through. Mintel's report states:

> '... there is the potential for commercial practice to be re-written such that some kind of charity association could become a more common element of brand marketing strategy ...'

Over time, as this becomes an established part of companies' marketing mix, differentiation will diminish and the impact of such an association will be reduced. But the good news is that right now there is huge opportunity for charities to persuade companies there is real potential in linking up with good causes.

Interestingly, men, those who are professionals and managers, and consumers from London and the south are more likely to associate companies with good causes. People who are labourers or unemployed are least likely to make the link, showing, perhaps a greater distrust of business motives.

Mintel have provided real research flesh on the bones of instinct and private success that companies and fundraisers have experienced. Prior to this report, some surveys commissioned by individual charities and campaign results had suggested that consumers responded well to cause related promotions. One figure often touted was that in product promotions, if faced with broadly similar brands where one has a charity link, 70% of the time the consumers will buy the linked product.

There are warnings here as well. The respondents to Mintel had only heard of two CRM campaigns – Tesco's Computers for Schools and the Andrex association with Guide Dogs for the Blind. One is not associated with the charitable sector; the other is an obvious association with previous Andrex campaigns.

What companies think of charities

Due to Mintel research, for almost the first time, we can tackle company bosses with real market intelligence from what is probably the UK's leading analyst of consumer markets. This is important, as anything and everything we do in this marketplace must be professional. Outside the top national and multinational corporations, who may be aware of this background rise of the ethical consumer and the US experience, local company views about the level of professionalism in the voluntary sector are remarkably consistent. The evidence is of course, anecdotal, but many regional fundraisers will tell you the same story.

'Charities? Oh yes, run by folks with pony tails and Jesus sandals – and that's just the men … Those who couldn't cut it in the real world … who reject profit, until they want a slice for their ne'er do wells … amateur and out of touch with the world of business …'

Although this is an exaggeration, what you must understand is there is some element of this prejudice in most companies you will deal with. It is vital that you do nothing in your contact or approach to prove it right. Yet we frequently do make simple mistakes that demonstrate how little some of us understand the corporate world.

Take timing of approach. For example, if a company financial year runs from April to April, then the bulk of its planning decisions on budgeting expenditure are taken the previous autumn. Once these lines and plans are down in the budget paperwork, then changes are often very difficult to achieve. Yet time and time again charities ring up companies in March or April to talk about this summer's events, demonstrating from the very beginning that they do not understand how companies work. If you are looking for quick cash, sponsorship is not for you.

Timing

Sponsorship fundraising is a medium-term activity. If your organisation decides to start a sponsorship campaign today, it should not expect real results for around 18 months. That is a fact of life in this market, not because I say so, but because that is how corporate budgets work.

Sponsorship and the marketing mix

Clearly, from a company point of view, with the Mintel research and the US experience as a backdrop, sponsorship (and the wider cause-related marketing) is set to become an accepted and effective part of the marketing mix. Few companies rely on only one advertising or marketing tactic, and most use a mixture of techniques to promote their market and their product. Companies cannot, and do not, operate in a world divorced from social concerns. Their success will often depend on how well they communicate and interact with all of the groups that may impact on their business environment, not just customers, but perhaps also shareholders, investment managers, employees, and decision makers at both national and local levels. Sponsorship is and can be aimed quite specifically at any one of those groups.

For most companies sponsorship is seen to fit mainly at the public relations end of the marketing mix. A survey amongst members of Arts & Business indicated 50% of company decisions about sponsorship were made in PR departments. This is reflected by the fact that success of sponsorship activities is often measured by name recognition, media comment, and not through direct links to sales figures.

With this emphasis on PR you will have to prove to the potential sponsor that your organisation is capable of managing the media coverage element. You will need to show past examples of coverage and media releases. You must also tackle one of the great fears that sponsoring companies have – that media organisations will drop the sponsors name from the title of the event.

● SPONSORSHIP SAGA

For all of us it was a big deal. £10,000 to sponsor three events over two years, and an option to renew for a further three years if successful. After the first event – which went superbly – to our horror we found the sponsor's name dropped from press coverage.

When I took this up with the editor, she told me it was the newspaper's policy not to provide free advertising – she had a whole department selling that at a price. I asked her if this reporting wasn't a breach of accuracy – using only part of the name of the event. I asked her how she squared her views with the sports pages – littered with local pubs which sponsored teams and tournaments. Why should social sponsorship, probably more desirable to the community as a whole, be treated differently? Did she have the right to deprive local consumers of the choice between responsible companies and others?

She didn't agree; she didn't concede. But the sponsor's name was in the next reporting and that saved both the deal and the extension for us.

This is a real issue which is usually more difficult on local radio and television than in newspapers. Sports and the arts have struggled with the same problems, but now find that sponsors' names are routinely included in coverage. The Carling Premier League and the Cornhill Tests have blazed trails for all of us.

NOW DECIDE:

- *What type of local presence can you find?*
- *Can you prove CRM principles to executives?*
- *Can you wait 18 months for real return?*
- *Do you understand the principles of the marketing mix?*

---

3 Preparing your organisation

$\bullet$

- *Is sponsorship the best way of raising the funds?*
- *Is the whole charity ready for the trials of a sponsorship campaign?*
- *What range of groups does your charity reach?*
- *Are there potential ethical difficulties?*

Are you ready for sponsorship?

The very first step in developing a sponsorship strategy is to take a cold, hard and honest look at your own organisation. Sponsorship is not and never will be money earned easily. It is a long and hard road to winning the sponsor in the first place, and it is quite difficult and time consuming to manage the relationship effectively and positively when the business is won. Sponsorship will only work if it is given the necessary staff time and the support of the whole organisation.

There are some traditional complaints found in many charities. They form a sort of closed loop of thinking that limits the ability to manage wider relationships like sponsorship. The 'closed loop' goes something like this:

1. We are doing good and important work.
2. Money will always be a problem, as the wider community doesn't appreciate how important our work is.
3. We dare not look three to five years ahead – we must focus on winning grants for next year or we won't be here.
4. Anyway, our work is tied to grant makers' priorities and timescales.
5. Companies have lots of money, and ought to support our good and important work.
6. But they don't – so we're grant dependent.

7. So our staff are paid less than they're worth …
8. We're dependent on volunteers, who are great, but …
9. So we can't run projects as well as we'd like to.
10. However, … (back to 1)

If this sounds like your organisation, stop any sponsorship plans now. Unless and until you can change that view, your organisation will not be ready to enter a serious sponsorship relationship. Go out in the world of sponsorship with those attitudes, and you'll fail dispiritingly to win any support (which will reinforce the whole group's self-righteous view of point 5!) and worse, you'll mess up the market for the rest of us who know what we're doing. Instead, sit down with a sheet of paper and ask yourself the following questions. Then ask them again of your boss, others in the organisation and the trustees.

Is sponsorship the best way of getting the cash you need?

Sponsorship only works if it is one strand in a sensible fundraising strategy for the whole organisation. It is also less about money than it is about linkage between the charity and the company – the cause and the product or service. Yet money – or usually the lack of it – will often drive a sponsorship campaign by a charity.

I have been training charities in the process of winning sponsorship support for more than a decade, and I swear bookings on the courses rise each year after the two weeks or so of television exposure for the Embassy World snooker championship held at the Crucible Theatre Sheffield each year. I have this image of charity chief executives across the country sitting watching large cheques handed out to snooker players and thinking 'I'll have a slice of that!'

In fact the first requirement of a sponsorship relationship is financial credibility. Successful, financially-sound organisations will win sponsorship support more easily. There is no way any company will commit its resources and name to an organisation that is hand-to-mouth in managing its finances. Most companies' short-term budget decisions are on the timescale seen as long-term by closed loop charity thinkers. If you need cash sooner than 18 months away; if you aren't prepared for long-term commitment; if you haven't already exhausted or exploited fully more established forms of fundraising, think again. Company sponsorship cannot be for deficit fundraising, plugging gaps, or a last resort. It has to be a positive strategy for your whole organisation.

Is the charity suitable for sponsorship?

Trustees and chief executives can lead charity fundraisers to despair. Too often, they approach sponsorship from the wrong end, by pondering what they would like funded. The focus of their attention is their own need for money, not what the potential sponsor's needs are. We usually see this at its most basic – and possibly ludicrous – when we encounter the sad fundraiser who has been instructed to get a sponsor for the annual report. This seems to be a specialist dead end of closed thinking, guaranteed to fail.

- We have to produce an annual report.
- This is time consuming and relatively expensive.
- So let's get a sponsor to offset the cost.

All of which begs the obvious question – how many of your supporters, staff and volunteers actually, willingly, read your annual report? The parts of your organisation's work that are sponsorable are those that have *reach*, *impact* and *image*. Few smaller charity annual reports fulfil those criteria. Indeed few large charity annual reports fulfil those criteria. So perhaps they don't need to be quite so expensively produced? And if you are successful in getting your real work funded by a judicious mix of fundraising techniques, then you will probably find the money to produce an annual report when you need to. A newsletter; project-linked campaign material; curriculum-linked educational packs; signage on project sites; logos on staff uniforms – all may have better reach and impact than the annual report. Think about the sponsor's needs first, then what you can offer to meet them. And you'll notice even in that short, off-the-cuff list, events don't get a mention either. You can surprise a potential sponsor by relegating events to a position low down your list, as it's where they always expect you to start!

To help assess whether your charity's activities have the *reach*, *impact* and *image* necessary for sponsorship, ask yourself the following questions.

Who do we reach?

Adults, children under 16, in school or out of school, students (16–22 years), schools, colleges, universities, businesses, consumers (by category, what do your supporters or clients buy?), motorists, commuters, volunteers, supporters (may have some strong views in common), local authority decision makers, service providers, contract purchasers, government representatives, MPs, Lords etc., patrons and/or large supporters with influence, householders are just some of the possible answers. Beneficiaries and service users should not be omitted from this list. For many years charities and companies have, to some extent, dismissed clients in sponsorship package terms. But Mintel's CRM research identifies benefit claimants as amongst the most likely to switch their spending to a charity-linked product.

Most charities reach or influence a far wider range of people than they at first give themselves credit for. Try this little exercise. On a blank sheet of paper place your charity in the middle – then add arrows and circles for the different – and varied – publics you may have contact with. A public is defined as any group of people who may have an interest in or impact on the charity. You may end up with something like this.

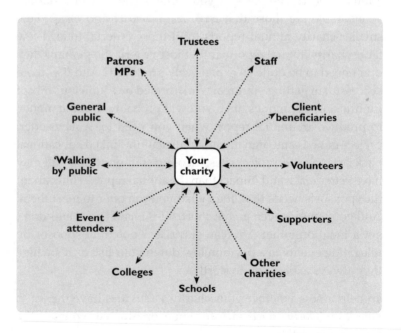

How do we reach them?

For example, the 'walking by' public may see a sign over the door of your building, on the sides of a vehicle, on your roof if it is overlooked by a railway line. There is a marvellous tale of an enterprising fundraiser who merely 'sold' his organisation's roof to an advertiser each year, because it lay directly under the flight path of the city's main airport! Not too many ethical problems either – nobody from the charity ever went up to the roof to see the advert!

In schools you may reach children, parents and teachers through educational material, guides and maps. In the media it could be through press release material, editorial coverage, or your own advertising. You may be known to those in the local authority through letter headings, attendance at events and information leaflets. You may reach beneficiaries, simply through the knowledge and goodwill generated by your work.

Why do we reach them?

What influence do we have? And perhaps, therefore, what do they think of us? For example, if your supporters are used to receiving 'death or glory' appeals from you because there's never enough money, they will almost certainly see you as a good and worthy cause, but financially a little chaotic! If you then set up a sponsorship deal with an insurance company, it probably won't work. Your implicit endorsement of their trustworthiness and investment returns won't carry much weight with your supporters and so your sponsor is unlikely to get value for money from the deal. Considering the fact that about a third of the sponsorship market is banking and finance product linked, financial credibility is going to be important.

Whoever your sponsor is, from their point of view your charity needs to have a good reputation with its supporters, in order for the company to reap the benefits of your implicit endorsement. Our attitude towards the media may be double-edged, but a good working relationship with them is vital. We reach many people through media coverage of our activities, if our events are interesting enough to attract the media in the first place. The publicity raises our profile which makes us more appealing to companies.

Each of the groups we reach will have a view on our effectiveness and integrity as an organisation – and that will help us assess why we reach them, and what influence we may have over them.

When do we contact them?

Sponsorship works at its best when it enhances or is added to an existing contact, rather than being the purpose of the contact.

 SPONSORSHIP SAGA

I met representatives from two charities recently who had accepted business sponsors whose sole purpose was to effect solid introductions to local MPs. The first immediately wrote to its two linked MPs, introducing the sponsor, informing them that the sponsor would be in touch about its forthcoming (and unconnected to the charity) lobbying campaign. Neither MP replied, but forewarned, when the company approached, issued standard, written replies. The second invited the MP to give out prizes at a forthcoming event, ensured that it was sponsored by the company, and that the PR department was there for the pictures and a chat over a drink afterwards. I overheard them fixing a luncheon date. I don't know the result, but which company do you think got the better hearing and spent its money more wisely? The second charity made the initial contact with the MPs in the context of a suitable event, which in turn eased the way for the sponsors.

Some of you, by now, will be thinking the idea that a company can buy access to an MP through your goodwill is disgraceful. If this is the case you might as well go back to the closed loop at the start of the chapter and stay with grants. It may not always be as blunt and blatant as this, but a sponsor will always be seeking influence, contact, image, or change in behaviour from somebody associated with your organisation. That's what the interchange of mutual benefit actually means. If you don't like it, don't do it – and don't get paid for it.

Sponsorship demands patience and long-term planning, whether your target audience is young people, the disabled or MPs. It is vital to organise an activity that not only attracts the specific group, but also matches the image of the charity with that of the company.

Where do they live (and purchase)?

Sponsorship works best with a tight geographical and/or decision–maker market that we can identify. Remember that each of those groups of people is potentially a centre of influence for another group such as their family, work colleagues, friends, church congregation. Your influence may be less as you get further from the centre, but it may still extend wider than your immediate contacts.

Can you meet the demands of a sponsorship relationship?

One of the things that most often goes wrong in sponsorship activity is the relationship during the life of the deal. Establishing sponsorship as an income for your organisation is an investment. Like all investments there is an initial outlay, a degree of risk and probably, low returns in the early years. In many charities, cash-stretched and understaffed, this is extraordinarily difficult. But it is vitally important that when the deal is won there is still sufficient time allocated by managers to deliver the promised benefits. This genuinely reaches across the whole organisation. Message taking, speed of response, receptionist and telephonist approaches to their work, good teamwork, genuine awareness of the sponsor and their needs are all vital. You are trying to establish that you are a credible professional, commercial partner. Here's a list of the top 10 points to ponder.

1. Listen to the message on your answer machine – is it friendly and informative? Not got an answer machine? Get one. Also consider a mobile phone and/or pager. Commercial partners expect prompt responses.

2. Go out one lunchtime, call your office and leave a complicated message with an unspellable (probably Polish or Russian) name for yourself. How your call was treated and greeted and how accurate the message is will tell you much!

3. Greet visitors and callers warmly. Be helpful and friendly and smile even if you're not pleased to see them.

4. Get a colleague or friend who works in the commercial world to call and visit you. Keep them waiting for 10–15 minutes, then listen carefully to their observations afterwards. How were they treated? Were they given coffee? What was there

available to read – was it current or out-of-date and dog-eared? What do they now know about your organisation's work and the private lives of your receptionist and their friends, having listened to the (sometimes careless) conversations? How professional do they now view your organisation as being?

5. When that colleague reaches your office/work space get them to stop and describe exactly what they see. Is it cramped, untidy and chaotic (I should confess here – that precisely describes my own personal way of working, which is one reason why I work for myself!), or does it look purposeful and orderly, however small? Similarly, take that colleague into your meeting room, if you have one, for the same review.

6. Look carefully at your letterhead and current information leaflets. I know we live in an age where almost anyone can produce their own letterhead on a DTP system – but too often it looks like something an eight year old produced and nobody had the heart to change! Your letterhead and leaflets strike a tone and image. Is it the right one?

7. Seek out a charity supporter from the commercial world, and talk to them about their honest opinion of your organisation, its image, strengths and weaknesses. Then be aware of how to sell those strengths and re-shape those weaknesses.

8. Call a staff meeting, to share your findings and explain how important these things are for the sponsorship marketplace.

9. Dress the game. Whilst dress code in the commercial world is not what it was, don't arrive for a meeting looking like their worst expectations.

10. Don't forget that hospitality elements may be an important element of the sponsorship package. Would you entertain at your charity's offices? If not, accept from the start that hotel costs may be part of your investment.

Is the company the right partner for you?

This is the hardest question of all. It is all too easy to arrange deals with companies whose ethics and/or product and services may cause offence to your supporters and damage your image. Often the sort of companies that are in the marketplace seeking social sponsorship are doing so in order to move from a dubious image towards that of a good corporate citizen!

Many charities tie themselves in huge, tortuous knots over the business of ethics. Tobacco is out, now by choice, soon by law; exploitation of workers overseas is out; dubious marketing practices and environmentally-unfriendly attitudes can also restrict your choice. In fact it is all too easy to write an ethical policy which ensures you can't talk to any company at all. I have found in my conversations with some charities that ethics is a huge issue before or just as they start looking for sponsorship, but that views become more sharply pragmatic as deals follow and cheque sizes are balanced against potential risk. Although obviously you don't want to alienate your supporters or adversely affect your image, you too will probably find that your organisation as a whole is more comfortable with sponsorship once they have some experience of it.

NOW DECIDE:

● *Can you, and your colleagues, cope with a sponsorship relationship?*

● *Who does your charity message reach?*

● *Has your charity got a credible, professional image?*

● *Will your supporters tolerate the ethical risks of sponsorship?*

---

4 How to approach a potential sponsor

- *What's the most effective form of approach?*
- *Is there anybody out there who can help?*
- *Who's the most effective person to start with?*
- *Do you have to meet?*

The initial approach

However much time you spend preparing your own organisation, you reach that awful moment when you have to step outside and enter the marketplace. It is somehow nicer, easier, and sometimes argued to be more professional, to make the first approach by letter. It is far too easy to talk yourself out of making the initial telephone call, especially if you believe that all charities are used to paperbound approaches; that it's how their main contacts with companies have been conducted when seeking money; and that the telephone is only for selling double glazing. However, if you want to fail, rely on writing letters, and getting no replies. Companies are often flooded with written applications for their sponsorship budgets, most of which are inappropriate to the company's needs. If you write to a company, you will have to provide some information about what you have in mind and you will be guessing the company's interests.

Sponsorship is only successfully bought face to face. The whole of your initial activity should be focused solely on getting in to see the right person in the company. There are only two sensible ways to do that.

Personal contact

Opening doors into relevant companies is eased considerably if you can use approaches through personal contacts. At this point many of you will switch off, with negative thoughts like:

(a) personal approaches are for big charities who know famous people
(b) we don't know famous any people, so
(c) it won't work.

However, no organisation ever operates in a social and economic vacuum. Indeed the whole basis of sponsorship approaches to companies depends on the concept of contact with society. Why then, would you presume that your organisation operates in such a vacuum? Part of the last chapter got you to look hard at your publics – people you are in touch with. Amongst those there are potential introducers. Each of those is a possible centre of influence who may know others in companies that could help you. Ask yourself the following questions.

Do you have a patron?

And before you say yes, I mean a *working* patron. For many charities patrons are RHINOs – Really Here In Name Only! Indeed charities are often so pleased that Lord so & so, or the MP or whoever takes an interest in their work, that the first words out of their mouths can be, 'We won't take much of your time!' Approach patrons quite clearly with the intention of asking them for between four and six hours' work each month. That work will usually consist of discussing lists of names with them – who they know. People recruited as patrons still tend to be drawn from the same strata of society as trustees of charitable trusts, directors of businesses, and decision makers in local and sometimes national government.

Charities want these people as patrons, so others will look at their organisations and say, 'Well if *they* approve of their work, the charity must be legit!'. For most charities, there are two kinds of supporter – the committed individual who wholeheartedly believes in the work; and the individual who supports the work because they are asked to do so by someone whose opinion they trust. This is exactly why direct mail approaches often depend heavily on a message from a well-known and/or respected individual.

A patron can fulfill that latter role on a personal level, and open doors for you across local and regional businesses. They are not selling the concepts and approaches, merely telling appropriate people that it is worth talking to you. They are also saying, 'Trust me, I have an association with this charity, and it's worth a bit of your time'.

If not a patron, a group of askers?

When charities undertake major fundraising activity they will often develop a small sub-group of askers who are willing to represent them to a wider range of people. In exactly the same way, a development committee of powerful and influential people can be put together to open doors for you. This is a hard but necessary prerequisite to a successful search for sponsorship.

 SPONSORSHIP SAGA

It was the germ of a simple idea that came up in discussion over coffee one evening. One of our supporters, who was also a governor of a local school, told me how the prospective MP had recently joined the governing body. His zeal and enthusiasm and comments on every agenda item added, on average, an extra hour to each meeting.

A good story. It made me chuckle, but then my brain kicked into gear and I, too, contacted the constituency office. In the year before the election we garnered three personal appearances, and a handful of introductions to groups and companies he met on the campaign trail.

The election duly came and went. He won. He's so busy right now we just get apologies and fine words. He's resigned from the governing body — they're quite pleased to reduce the length of their meetings again.

However, all is not lost. The ex-sitting MP that didn't get elected needs to re-build their links to the community, so perhaps I should call their constituency office?

For the smaller charity, start with local councillors and industrialists, or even those aiming to be local councillors, or those who've been local councillors and recently lost their seat. Think of your publics again. Volunteers in your organisation may have jobs in local companies. Alternatively, paid staff may have partners or friends that could act as introducers. Think of all the contacts you have already and then target powerful individuals who you think would like to support you in the future. Once you have decided who you wish to approach, invite them to an event, following that invitation with a meeting and discussion.

This is not as hard as it sounds. There are many in the community who like to be seen to help charitable activity. The vital thing for you to remember is that you remain the conductor by guiding, enthusing and cajoling your committee members to action. They have real jobs and their own lives as well, so you must keep their work for you in the forefront of their mind. These individuals can in part be drawn from existing supporters, but it is also important to bring in some new blood and new thinking.

● SPONSORSHIP SAGA

The telephone call caught us on the hop. The executive who was coming down asked if it was OK to bring his mother, who was heading home, 150 miles the other side of our project. Of course, we said yes. And then wondered what we were going to do with mother while we made our pitch.

Eventually we called on Irene – a local supporter who'd run the odd coffee morning for us. She took mother shopping to the best local haunts; for a real cream tea; and a tour of the best local sights – including five minutes with the Mayor.

As I waved an ecstatic mother farewell, I almost felt sorry for the executive, for whom our meeting had gone well, but not perfectly. 150 miles of 'They were very nice people, are you going to work with them, will I see them again … ?'.

Monday morning brought a telephone call and the negotiation of a three year £12,000 deal … and his mother's coming to cut the ribbon!

Can you run a development evening?

Often the search for sponsorship contacts will begin with a series of development evenings. These events should be specially designed for a number of specific guests, with meeting and greeting in mind. You can organise one with the help of your development group, and follow it up with a series of meetings with prospective sponsors. A development evening may be a dinner, a drinks party in a patron's home, or any activity where mixing and chatting is amongst the main aims of the evening. Business people understand the 'rules' of these invitations. If they accept and come along, they know they are likely to be asked to assist in some way. And remember – partners are important here.

Make the event invitations 'with partner'. If the partner has a great time, then they will ask when they'll be seeing such an event again. It puts an unsubtle and effective pressure on their other half to keep involvement going!

What about your trustees/management committee?

In spite of all the hard work done by many trustees, there are still a number of 'committee sitters' on charitable boards. If you want to get rid of them, then start putting them on the spot. Talk to them about using their resources and contacts to further the search for sponsorship by the charity. In discussion, most will agree, but do nothing. Some will dispute that they know anybody useful. All will do nothing unless you follow it up. Give them each a sheet of paper full of prompts to make them think. Who do they work for? Which local businesses do they use and are well known to? Where do their neighbours work? What other organisations do they work for? Who else serves with them on those bodies? When put under pressure in this way, 'committee sitters' will hopefully spring into action, or retreat pretty quickly.

Make no mistake, personal approaches work the best. It really is worth putting energy, effort, and money into finding the right types of personal contact. If you can't or you won't, then you'll have to resort to the telephone.

The telephone

Those readers who shrank from the idea of personal contact will probably now be on the verge of tears. Unless you make personal contact work, you now have to do it the hard way. If the thought of cold calling terrifies you, before you give up the idea of sponsorship entirely, put yourself in the company contact's shoes. They are regularly pitched on the telephone for all sorts of sales opportunities – for most business people telephone sales

● SPONSORSHIP SAGA

We decided to cultivate sponsorship contacts through a series of development evenings. There were two basic choices – either to invite a number of possible sponsors to an existing event or run specific events for the cultivation process. In the end, we tried both. They had advantages and disadvantages. By inviting a smaller number to an existing event I could get to speak to each special attender personally – but the event may not lend itself to easy conversation! With the specially designed events, talking time is built in but I found it hard to personally meet each sponsorship prospect.

Over the course of a year we issued 200–300 invitations, and got 70 of those prospects along for an event. Of those, ten became real sponsorship possibilities for the next financial year.

What we did learn en route? Simple, common sense things. Initially, potential sponsors judge your abilities as a potential partner by the nature of the event, the quality of the invitation, timescale (their diaries are busy) and where the event is held. Having a sponsor for the event itself is a good touch, but the venues themselves shouldn't be too grand or the potential sponsors will feel you don't need the money. Equally, the event usually shouldn't be at your charity HQ, which is rarely grand enough. The exception here may be to invite one or two sponsors to an open evening about your work, but I have to say these are easier to sell to grant makers than to sponsors!

Don't forget the little touches. A special welcome on arrival and a discreet marker such as a buttonhole – name badges can look silly. A finger buffet with a drink, and a sensible hosting policy – perhaps one host each to two or three couples will help keep the flow of gentle information and good impression flowing.

Debrief the hosts straight after the event. Comments, views expressed, all should be noted for use in follow-up phone calls. Those phone calls are to establish that they enjoyed the evening, and to follow through with a meeting to discuss possible mutual opportunities. That's what we were after – we got enough to make it worthwhile – but it cost £2,500 to achieve. In the medium term a reasonable investment for our charity; but at the start hard to justify!

approaches are a way of life. You feel much less comfortable with this than they do!

Think about the competition for this budget. Advertising is regularly pitched for by telephone, not only in the first instance, but often without a formal meeting at all! Don't try to compete by pitching for a deal on the phone. For you, the basics here are very simple. You are pitching for a meeting. Without a meeting, sponsorship won't happen. You may find that when you do talk to prospective sponsors on the telephone, they will not want to meet. Their time is valuable, and they will want you to put something in writing before they can meet you. You must resist this, as before you can propose a sponsorship package that is right for the company you will need some information.

But already we presume you're talking to the right person, which can be hard to achieve. If there's no published name to talk to – and there often isn't – you have to start by asking the telephonist or receptionist who might be the appropriate person to speak with. Clearly, people have done this quite frequently and some companies will simply not divulge names over the phone. In which case, start with the marketing manager's PA or equivalent; don't go straight to the manager themselves. The PA's job is to control access to the relevant decision maker, and they are initially possibly your best friend. If the PA tells you that they've tried sponsorship and it didn't work, or they don't do it – they're probably right. If they're neutral or content with the idea, push on and ask for a telephone appointment with the decision maker.

One very well-known city headhunting firm quite deliberately keeps you waiting 23 minutes for your appointment. When you are invited in, the headhunter pauses for a word with the PA. They have found, over time, that the best candidates are relaxed, and friendly with every level within a company. The PA's impression of you is the first recorded, and most important, first hurdle.

Are you convinced yet? The PA is more than a conduit to the decision maker. They will usually decide if you get through at all, and will often colour the judgement of the decision before you even reach them. Any comment about you from the PA to the decision maker can make or break your proposal.

Work with the PA, find a mutually convenient time to phone and talk to the decision maker, and book it in their diary as a telephone appointment. This is an effective trick. A timed phone call, noted in your and their diaries, lifts your call above standard telephone selling routine. You must make the call at the agreed time, so clear your space that day. If the decision maker is going to be out, the PA will call and re-arrange your time.

● SPONSORSHIP SAGA

When I set out to hunt for sponsorship, I was strong on only discussing anything with decision makers. With some companies it took four or five attempts – they were always busy. When I got in to see one executive she told me with some amusement that this was her PA's way of making people aware of relative values. She also told me the story of how all of the middle and senior managers in the company had attended an outward bound team-building course. You know the sort of thing – blisters, booze, tears and friendly hugs while getting cold and wet on an inhospitable moor!

They were away four days – the factory ran smoothly and there were no real difficulties. Upon their return, the managers agreed their PAs and assistants would benefit from a similar experience. The manager's course was seven years ago. They're still waiting for the moment that the PAs can be all spared! I was very polite to her PA on the way out.

But, of course, the really big question is what you're going to say! This is difficult. Every single one of us has been pitched at some point by a telephone sales person working from a script … and resented it! So you have to sound relaxed and spontaneous, responding individually to the questions that will naturally arise. Seasoned campaigners' advice tends to focus on what not to get drawn into – i.e. discussing the type of event or activity, costs, media coverage, or proposals in any detail. What you must understand is that as soon as you say, 'We were thinking about getting sponsors for our Quiz Evening' they'll say, 'We don't do events!' This is all a bit of a game. Most times, if you provide any detail, they're given an excuse not to see you. The trick is to convince the executive to spare time to meet you.

How to fix a meeting

From the very first moment you start to talk, plug the meeting. After the introductions, start with words such as, 'I'm arranging meetings with local companies to discuss sponsorship opportunities that have proved to be successful marketing initiatives for companies elsewhere in the UK. Could you spare some time to meet with me on Tuesday or Thursday of next week?' This type of talk may be alien to you as a charity, but you have to prove that you're capable of commercial partnership here, and that you're not just another charity coming cap-in-hand. These are busy people and they appreciate those who are up front about what they need. Remember that they're pitched like this very often, so this technique surprises them less than it surprises you!

Responses, of course, vary widely, but fall into distinct categories:

Q What makes you think our marketing's suitable for use with yours?

A Until we meet, I don't. Until we meet and can discuss your and our market profiles, I don't. Until we meet I don't know if you can use sponsorship as part of your marketing mix. I do know other companies have done so successfully. Which do you prefer, Tuesday or Thursday?

Q You're wasting your time, we've spent our budget for this year.

A Good. I wouldn't expect to come and discuss this year's activity anyway. Marketing initiatives like this have to be planned as part of the whole year's budget to get full benefit. And that's usually at least a year ahead ... so which is best, Tuesday or Thursday?

Q What's the rush if it's for next year?

A Because I need to get some information from you to draw up a detailed proposal to fit with your marketing objectives. That takes a bit of time before it can be submitted for your decision. The earlier we start, the easier that process is – did you say Tuesday was good?

Q Better put something on paper to me.

A That's the whole point of meeting. After that meeting I can send you a detailed proposal to fit your marketing plan. Thursday's better then?

Q Why should I bother to market with a charity?

A Because the polls tell us customers like it. I can show you those detailed figures when we meet. Is morning or afternoon better for you?

Q You need our donations manager.

A No I don't. This is a marketing proposition, with a bit of PR thrown in. It's not a request for a grant. Thursday afternoon then, about 3 o'clock?

The general idea here is that each objection is turned to a hinted-at advantage, to be explained more fully at the meeting. This process is just like applying for a job. When you first fill out the application form, your intention is to get an interview, then at successive stages to reach the final shortlist, and to get the job. So it is here that the meeting/interview must be secured as a vital stage in the process, and you must achieve it before you can pass on. Occasionally you get an exasperated …

Q You're so hung up on meeting – why? My time is valuable!

A I appreciate your time is valuable. However our experience of this marketplace clearly shows that sponsorship is never achieved without the two parties meeting and discussing possibilities. That's the meeting I'm hung up on, and I hope you'll meet with me next week …

The key underlining themes here are:
- You have some experience of this marketplace.
- That experience is on offer.
- It's been successful elsewhere (you can substitute that with 'locally' when you have a track record!).

Q How much is this going to cost me?

A Initially nothing except your meeting time. We will negotiate an appropriate fee according to the benefits you will get as part of the detailed proposal.

In the end, many will say no, some will say yes, and some will say maybe. If they say no, thank them for their time, wish them well and sign off. Remember this is a numbers game – you will get a lot of refusals and you must treat them with respect. As you have approached them rather than the other way round, they are under no obligation to say yes! If they do say yes, you'll have an appointment to prepare for.

Before the first meeting

Firstly, do a *little* research on the company. Read through their last annual report and take a swift look at recent press cuttings mentioning them (the internet is a great source for these!). This will be enough background information, as you will obtain most relevant information at the forthcoming meeting.

Secondly, do write and confirm the meeting. This is both a matter of professional courtesy, and an additional opportunity to enhance the impression you make on your opposite number. The letter itself should be brief and polite: thank them for their time already given on the telephone, confirm the time and date of meeting, and tell them how much you're looking forward to it.

Now you have a chance to send something with the letter that will improve your chances of closing the deal when you meet. Let's start with what *not* to send first. Many smaller charities, and some larger charities, will send an annual report and accounts or the current general information leaflet about the charity. Even worse, it could be the left-over appeal literature from last year which the boss insists must be used up before more money is spent to print any more!

None of these will make the right impression. They are written with general fundraising and donors in mind, and their tone will hinder, not help in this marketplace. Either you must have something that is specifically written for this market – I thoroughly commend the brochures printed as appendices here – or a simple 'patchwork' of press stories stapled to the back of your letter. This leaves the prospect knowing you understand the types of impact they will look to achieve from sponsorship – and that you do get some press coverage for your work. You will need a licence from the Newspaper Licencing Agency (see Resources) and permission from each publisher to use press cuttings in this way.

One last tip. A couple of lines in a letter, a photocopied sheet attached – there's still a chance the PA will simply tell their boss you've written confirming and not show them the letter. Put a handwritten PS on the bottom of the letter, asking the boss to thank the PA for all their help with the telephone appointment etc. It is very unusual for the PA not to show the boss the letter in those circumstances.

Some readers will think this is really cheap. As you read this book there will be many moments when you say 'I can't do that!' I can't make you do these things – I can only tell you of some of the ideas I've seen work in winning sponsors. Monitor those moments when you say 'I can't do that!' Often you really mean 'I won't do that!' which may explain why your charity's sponsorship programme is in the doldrums. Just try it – or you may be risking being successful!

There will be some companies who say 'maybe'. Experienced sales people of all descriptions will tell you that in the long term, the 'maybes' are often the best prospects. Their line of thought is probably as follows:

- Yes I can see the germ of a good idea here.
- But the current and planned budgets are committed.
- I have little time right now.
- Let's look at this when there's a serious chance of making it happen.

Your job is to ensure that interest doesn't die in the ensuing six months or however long they tell you to wait before you call back. Something must go to them every two months or so. A press report of a successful activity or event, with a brief (handwritten) comment on a compliments slip. The note should read something like, 'I know we agreed we wouldn't formally meet until November, but I wondered if this might be of interest'. Always stress the agreed month to meet. When that time arrives go back through the PA, the telephone appointment routine and start again. A good number of 'maybe' prospects will become sponsorship partners if you get this right, and they will usually provide larger sums of money for the first activity that they sponsor. The wait is nearly always worthwhile.

> ## Now decide:
> - Are you going to use personal contact?
> - Are you recruiting patrons and introducers?
> - Can you work with PAs and telephonists?
> - Can you make meetings happen?

5 Selling to a potential sponsor

● ●

> ● *What are the vital elements in preparing for a meeting?*
> ● *What type of presentation is best?*
> ● *Which information must be gathered?*
> ● *When will decisions be made?*

The first meeting

So you reach that crucial moment when you step into somebody's office and must live up to that professional image you've been working on since you started thinking about sponsors. At this point the classic error is to go with an activity or event in mind, present the merits of the idea, and hope they'll buy it. Instead, you must enter this first meeting intending to use it as an information-gathering exercise. Read that last sentence again and note the reference to 'first meeting'. Not only must sponsorship be bought face to face, but it will normally take at least two meetings. This first meeting is usually called the 'fact find' as you're going to gather all the information you need to go away and draw up a proposal that meets the sponsor's needs. Then you will return, present that proposal at the second meeting and close the deal. This meeting is usually called the 'present and close'.

None of this is as difficult as it sounds. Once you're in the meeting room (having done the 'handshake, hello, how's the weather, have a coffee' bit), then there is a moment's silence while you both take a deep breath, and then you're off. Often it is the manager, who is effectively hosting the meeting, who launches in, 'You said on the phone you have some useful marketing initiatives for me to consider ... '

This is the moment you've been working towards for many weeks. But this opportunity is not for selling the charity, or its good works. It is not about the event in three months' time that the boss is screaming at you to find a sponsor for. It is merely the next step in demonstrating to this individual that your organisation, albeit a charity, is a serious possible professional partner. The manager may still suspect that they will be pitched; that your style to date in getting this far is just a neat twist on a cap-in–hand approach. If that suspicion is confirmed, you will never recover or make this work.

What to ask

What you present now is the process: that this first meeting is to gather information, some of it quite specific, about the company, its market and objectives. Explain that you will then go and prepare a sponsorship report, recommending a type of activity, and return for a second meeting to go over the details.

Make no mistake. You are selling. Selling a reassurance that you are a serious competitor for advertising funds, and may have a genuine input to a successful marketing mix for the company. To some extent the terms 'fact find' and 'present and close' to describe the two meetings are misnomers. They imply that the selling is mainly undertaken at the second presentation/meeting. It isn't. If the first fact-find meeting is conducted properly, the second meeting is just to pick up the cheque. Virtually all of your selling – concept, personality, matching views, mutual interest – takes place during the fact-find conversation. The questions you ask, how you ask them, and how you manage the responses, will be key elements in this sale. So let's look at that first meeting, the information you *must* get, and how you can drag it out of reluctant executives.

Who are they selling to?

Who does this company see as the people and market they want to influence and be seen in? Not just right now but in 12–18 months' time when sponsorship deals may be truly up and running. This is a straightforward question for the executive: they know very clearly who their customer base is, and where the potential growth areas are. Listen carefully and note the answers. The whole point here is that you must be able to return with a proposal that has a good chance of reaching this group or groups of people. If you can foresee no possible link between their customer base and your publics, you should call a halt to the meeting and not waste your and their time.

If you think a proposal could target the company's customer base, an important supplementary question for you to ask is how the company reaches those groups now. This will help both you and the executive spot areas where sponsorship may fit neatly with other parts of the marketing programme. It also allows you to underline that sponsorship is more comfortably a marketing activity, and will need to be carefully coordinated with sales drives and programmes to achieve the best results for the company. This will be important later in the conversation when you look at measuring effectiveness and impact. Sales is an almost automatic element to consider for measuring impact – but you will have already established it is an imperfect link, as the success of sponsorship is more often assessed as part of the marketing mix, rather than by direct sales figures.

● SPONSORSHIP SAGA

A few years ago I decided to contact a well-known high street mother and baby retail chain. The charity I represented worked with under-fives, so I assumed that the company *must* be interested in this mutual marketplace. Imagine my disappointment when the marketing manager informed me that this wasn't the case and that they were working hard at marketing in the 5–11 year age group. They knew that mums to be and those with babies would come to their stores, but they lost them as customers when the children started school. Their aim was to market their school range of clothes and equipment, so families kept spending with them a little longer.

Your worst fear here is that the executive may say that their market is 'everybody', but this is not true. You're either being tested, or you're facing somebody who's going through the motions and not taking you seriously. Ask them to break it down, to describe the ideal customer. Tell them that according to Mintel, professionals, women, better-off families and affluent city-dwellers respond best to community sponsorship. Are those groups of interest to them?

You can't write a proposal on how to reach their customer unless you know who this is. And don't guess.

Unless you can discover who the company's customers are or will be, there is little point in finding out about …

Timescale

When does the company see an opportunity to use sponsorship in their marketing programme? Always look to the medium term. You've already assured them sponsorship needs to fit in with other marketing approaches and with sales drives and follow ups. This requires considerable coordination and planning, which cannot be rushed if it is to be successful. Executives are usually pleasantly surprised that you're not in a rush. Their experience of charities is that they are often desperate for money and very short-term in their view of raising it.

So tell them these deals take time to get right. Your time and effort is the charity's investment in ensuring a happy sponsor. In short, do it, as far as possible, to their timescale not yours – and that will usually mean planning for the next budget cycle if you want to win serious sums of money.

Type of activity

This is often the first big stumbling block. Ask the average executive what they can sponsor and the odds are they'll say, 'events'. That's what most of them see and expect of this marketplace. You must come prepared with a dozen different examples of sponsored activities, of which only one should be an event. Newsletters, whole projects, vehicles, buildings, advertising campaigns, staff uniforms, conference packs, identity badges, information packs, posters, banners, office equipment, folders, furniture, foyer space, food parcels – in short almost anything that has space for a company name that is seen by people can be sponsored. It is quite surprising what may carry a company name: a supermarket-sponsored lanyard at a Labour Party Conference, or a vodka brand on the flanks of cows near the London–Brighton railway!

Make yourself a page in a presentation file with passport-size pictures of images or actual sponsorship (landscape looks better than portrait). Under each picture give a few words of detail – 3,200 professionals in Rutland – about who will see each sponsorship element. The spread of your ideas and some knowledge of the markets they will reach will underline your professional approach. Take the executive past each picture; add a word or two of explanation, telling them that these are examples, not a full account of all that may be possible. After each explanation, ask if that sort of activity may be of interest to them.

When you get really good at this, you'll add one extra box at the top of the page – no picture, just a blank box with a question mark underneath it. Start your explanation to one side of it – proceed round the page and stop on the other side. Then wait. You'll soon learn, if you don't know already, that silence can be a powerful sales and negotiating tactic. The question about why the box is blank is obvious, and it is asked surprisingly often. Before you answer, remember how important personal input is to this business. Anything you can build into your structure that offers the executive the opportunity to contribute ideas will help make the deal much easier to close. When they do ask about the box, answer: 'That's for the sponsorship idea we haven't thought of yet, that will come from somebody like yourself', and smile. They'll smile; you'll all smile. It's a clever trick, but more than that it underlines the openness of the relationship that is being proposed – that magical two-way street of equals with mutual interest being served. This is not a cut and dried package, but something they can influence, help design and direct to ensure it meets their company needs as far as possible.

It is critical that you find an activity that sits comfortably not just with the required marketing reach, but also the company and its executives' image and interests. This will come from a matrix of their time, personal involvement, enthusiasm, responsibilities and other elements that you will probably never know. The easiest and most effective way is to offer the widest choice of opportunity and let them 'buy' the most appropriate areas.

Please do remember not to impose your choice and/or priority on them. There may, to you, be an obvious choice, direct to the necessary marketplace. But it may not fit with the company's other planned activities; they may have tried a similar approach before and failed; it may involve too much work for them personally; it may be too critical; or there may be any number of considerations, some of which may be uncomfortable to explain. So tread carefully. If you want to sell, sell to the client's perception of their priorities. It's their decision, so give them the space and respect to make it! If they're happy with their first experience, they may take your advice more easily on the second deal, when they know you can deliver.

Evaluation

There can be no serious proposal to win sponsorship without some discussion of how to measure the success of the deal. It's vital to discuss this before getting on to money, because this is perceived by the client as 'added value'. Relatively few companies will expect you to seriously discuss the impact of the sponsorship. It is notoriously difficult and often thought to be impossibly expensive to measure.

● SPONSORSHIP SAGA

The one thing I truly dreaded was discussing evaluation. I was expecting bar charts of column inches, colour coded calculations, and pages of percentages. What they wanted, in the end, was a reassurance that brand recognition had taken place.

I trotted off to the local college and spoke to the senior lecturer on the retail marketing course. Some questionnaires, free T-shirts and pencils brought a willing workforce of students eager to learn some basic marketing research techniques. Coming out of the sponsored event an impressive 98% of respondents interviewed by the students were brand aware, and 75% said they would be trying it soon.

Using the sponsoring company's name in the event title ensured newspaper mentions, and a very happy sponsor.

Evaluation may be imperfect, but it certainly helps build credibility and added value.

The number of responses to an insert in a magazine can be quantified, whether it be in terms of sales or enquiries generated. But the number of responses is meaningless unless it is set against the average response expected if a similar insert was placed in a similar magazine. An insert or advert in a sponsored newsletter may produce a 6.25% response. On its own, this figure may seem low to anyone unused to the response rates typical for direct marketing. If, however, a similar insert in a commercial publication usually produces a 5% response, and lacks the additional kudos of linking to charitable activity, then 6.25% becomes a useful figure.

Often companies will focus on media coverage. Before you become too weighed down in calculations of column inches, remember you only need a scandal involving royalty or a film star; an aeroplane crash; or locally, a divisive planning decision on out-of-town superstores, to throw your carefully laid plans out. It is imperative when you talk of media coverage that sustained campaigns with several opportunities for both media releases and photographs are part of the plan. Even then, use of the sponsoring company's name is at least as important as the size of the piece itself. Above all think photo opportunity. That is what brings the press along, that's what catches readers' eyes. And please be creative – every newspaper in the land could field several 'grip 'n' grin' (cheque handovers!) pictures every week.

Name recognition of the brand, company or product may be an important key. If the activity sponsored is an event, you could arrange brief interviews with some attenders as they leave. Talk to the local colleges about marketing courses, and if their students would like some practical market research experience. This will not only provide you with a willing workforce, but it also extends the potential impact of the sponsorship into a whole new area.

You need to find an evaluative tool that will match the company's aims, be it brand recognition or whatever. Then – and only then – can you talk about …

The fee

This is one of those points where the whole process threatens to unravel. Culturally, we British don't like to talk or haggle over price, but you must obtain this piece of information to be able to propose a sensible deal. Otherwise, you could return with a brilliant idea that would cost £5,000, and discover the company only wanted to spend £500. Or even worse, you could have a proposal for £500 and then discover they had £5,000 available.

The price of sponsorship depends on the value to the sponsor, not the cost to your charity, so it is not up to you to invent a figure. You must have, at the very least, a ballpark figure to work with from the executive. Make it a conditional question:

> 'If I can show you how to reach your target audience, in a manner that complements your existing approaches, in both time and style, properly evaluated – how much would you be willing to invest in such an opportunity?'

In an ideal world, they will tell you immediately, it will be more than you expected, and will be paid on time, every time! Unfortunately it is rarely this easy. Most times, a figure has to be coaxed from the executive and it can be as much fun as drawing teeth. From their point of view you still have to produce an idea that looks like it could really work, and convince them you can deliver it. If the executive commits too easily to a figure, it could make negotiating the best deal from you more difficult later on. But some sort of guide figure you must have.

Another selling trick might help. Have a wish list in your presenter file, a simple portrait page of prices, from a single named T-shirt at £50 at the top, with the price rising in stages, till you reach a brand new sponsored HQ building in the Home Counties at £2.75 million at the bottom of the page. Then ask your conditional question again – this time finishing with, 'Is this the sort of sum that may be available?' Then place your pen full on the page. A word of advice here: place your pen in the bottom half of the page on the more expensive items and whilst it will almost certainly be moved up, it will demonstrate that you mean business. In addition, remember charities often sell themselves and their wares too cheaply in sponsorship deals, so nudge them to realistic or worthwhile sums for you.

If you can't get at least a guide figure from them, stop the interview right there. Explain that everything you've seen and read about sponsorship tells you that a figure to work from is vital. Without that it's just too much guesswork for an effective proposal. If you have to, take a copy of this book with you, highlight this sentence, tell them I said a ballpark figure is a pre-condition of you writing a proposal. In short, the aim is to make a proposal that sells a deal with a scope to match the figure. Without this financial information, any proposal is a waste of time.

Date of next meeting

The process you are following now requires you to go away and prepare a proposal based on what you have learned about the company's expectations. At this point you should give the executive the opportunity to make some decisions. After so many questions, the executive is likely to be pleased to play a more active role in the process. Allow yourself 10–14 days to prepare the proposal, then ask them to pick a convenient day or time for the proposal to arrive. Ask them how many days they'd like to ponder the proposal, then ask for a firm second meeting.

This firm date is both good business practice – and a trial 'close'. Those unwilling to make second meetings until after getting the proposal are much less likely to buy. Their unwillingness tells us that something has gone wrong – they have not bought the concept. It is also axiomatic in a sales environment that you leave each meeting with something, albeit only a promise to listen to you again. Old hands at this type of work would tell you not to waste time drafting a proposal for someone who won't even commit to an appointment. If you don't believe them now, you will after writing to a few time-wasters. Get the date of next meeting in your diary *now*!

Are you the sole decision maker?

This is the real killer question as it requires the executive to admit the limit of their authority. Are they the organ grinder or the monkey? Do they make policy initiatives happen or just carry through others' ideas?

The safest way to achieve an answer is often to go back through the steps again, 'If we provide a vehicle to reach the right target audience to your timescale and budget, then when we meet again is there anything to stop the deal going ahead?' If other approvals will be needed, it is often now that you'll learn about them.

If this is to go to a committee for decision you've probably gone a step backwards in the process. You can offer to speak to them, but often it'll be refused. Many of these committees are private, internal groups. Do offer to send a personalised proposal to each member.

In the end, it may be better to scale down a deal to the level that the individual you're dealing with can authorise, than to go to an anonymous committee. A second deal, built on the success of the first when the committee has seen your work, may be a better bet. Be flexible and take a long-term view as it is much more likely to lead to success in the end.

You may already have some ideas from the meeting about specific events, or it may take your charity longer to choose the ideal activity. The trick is to use all the information you have gathered at this first meeting to make a decision. You will know what to avoid and the type of work the company will expect from you. Once you have taken into account all the information on target audience, timing, and fee expectation, you will be ready to write your proposal.

NOW DECIDE ... CAN YOU:

- *Focus on process before presentation?*
- *Ask all seven vital questions?*
- *Leave room for personal involvement from the executive?*
- *Find out who makes the real decision?*

---

6 The proposal

● *What sort of proposal works best?*
● *How much detail is needed?*
● *What is a 'fair' price?*
● *What benefits can be offered?*

Creating an image

The key element to remember when you write the proposal is the same as with every stage in this process. You have to create an image of a potential professional partner, concentrating on the commercial side of the deal, and presenting the business you're talking to with an irresistible opportunity. However, it is still possible to overdo it, to present such a glossy image that the company will somehow feel that money is being wasted. It is ironic, but amongst the double standards that you will meet in this marketplace is that, as a charity, you must be seen not to waste money at all. In part this is because the bulk of charity income is still felt by many to be not 'earned' but given, and should therefore be managed with exaggerated care.

The proposal must, somehow, bridge this gap. However good an impression you created at the meeting, it is the proposal that will be shown to others. These others will not have been exposed to all the various stages in the process that have allowed you to create the right partnership images, they will judge chiefly on the proposal.

So, the proposal must be able to strike that commercial, professional image, without being over-glossy or expensive. It is a good habit to think through a standard outline and basic layout to save time and effort. The same basic structure can be practised and refined, and remain formatted on the word processor, ready to be adapted to each proposal. The structure should be able to be used for both small and large deals. As with every other element in sponsorship, practice makes perfect. One possible format is shown here, but you must find your own comfortable approach that works and stick with it. The decisions are basic but important.

Bound style or letter?

Generally a bound proposal will look better than a letter and attachments. Indeed, with a bound proposal you may not have to send a formal letter at all. A handwritten compliments slip may be just as or more effective. The centre of attention must be the proposal, not the letter. It can be laid out to read quickly and easily, separating the main selling points page by page. A slide binder may be better than spiral binding as at the second meeting you can remove the binder and lay the sales process out step by step.

Are covers important?

In a bound proposal the cover or folder is going to be the initial element that strikes the reader and creates an image of your charity. Images can be striking, but be careful if you are using the charity logo or photographs, especially in a set of printed covers – they tend to date easily and you may have to re-print. Remember that the stress on the charity is not the main selling point. A classical or plain cover will not date easily. If you are stuck for ideas, a plain 'smoked glass' perspex cover over a card frontispiece with a cut space to reveal the name works well.

How many pages?

The proposal should consist of between five and seven sheets that can be read in five minutes or less. Do not forget that the proposal is essentially an executive summary of the process to date. Do not be tempted to push in every detail, with several appendices and a draft contract. It is an affirmation of what was learned and agreed in the first meeting. Once the proposal is with the company you can call and ask if any other detail is required, and send it on if it is.

What should it contain?

- A simple summary of discussions to date, including type of project to be sponsored.
- A complete listing of the benefits to the sponsor.
- The fee for this partnership.
- An outline marketing timeplan, giving major milestones and steps.
- A note on methods of evaluation.
- A brief page about the charity's work or supporters relevant to the deal.

This document should be dripping with the benefits of buying sponsorship, who the deal may impact upon or influence, and the enhanced image that may attach to the sponsor. It is *not* a sale of the charity's works and profile.

What follows is an example for you to work on and work with. It has been known to succeed! Only the names and places have been changed to protect the guilty.

You'll notice, first of all, that it contains photographs. These are essential, whether you scan them in on desktop publishing equipment, or just stick them on the page as originals. The photos are there for a purpose. Indeed the whole layout of this proposal is based on much of what is known about how people read. Photographs are the number one attention-grabbing device in print, and they set an image about what is on offer and what is being bought.

At the beginning of this proposal is a simple and short statement of what is offered and who already supports it. If you have won funds from charitable trusts and other companies then say so, as this can impress the reader. On balance, decision makers are much more likely to back an idea that another has already judged a good project or a good risk. Local companies appreciate local trust presence, and national companies value national trust presence.

It is deliberately drafted and written in the simplest of English. Good proposals pass the ten-year-old test. Before you send your proposal out, take it home and show it to your ten-year-old. (If you haven't got a ten-year-old, borrow one. In my experience there is usually one hanging about nearby.) If your average ten-year-old can get the basis of what you're selling you've got the level of English about right. That may sound absurdly cynical, but it is a simple recognition of a simple truth. A proposal understood at the first reading is more likely to succeed than something that requires huge effort on the part of the reader.

Check your proposal for simplicity: excise jargon; limit sentence length; limit paragraph length; leave white space clear on the page. You already have the benefit of knowing about the target audience, timing and fee expectation. So use this knowledge to create a clear and simple proposal.

The thrust and tone of this proposal is very straightforward. It represents the steps in the sales track from the concept through to investment. The sample contains the essential elements of any proposal, broken down into the following sections.

The Manchester Victoria Dock Centre Trust

SPONSORSHIP PROPOSAL FOR
MANCHESTER VICTORIA LIGHT RAILWAY

Freda Festival
Fundraiser

7th January 2000

The cover links the name of the potential sponsor and the charity in print for the first time. The names are over a positive upbeat image of charity clients at their best. This should be, if possible, the type of image PR people drool over. The whole image is positive and wholesome, emphasising good citizenship.

The use of the fundraiser's name is also quite deliberate. If sponsorship is best won face-to-face, underlining that individual relationship can't hurt.

Why Sponsor this Watersports Centre?

The Manchester Victoria Dock Centre Trust, based on the largest enclosed water sports space in the heart of the area served by the Manchester Victoria Light Railway (MVLR). The Centre provides access to water sports for local people from the surrounding areas – recognised as one of the most socially deprived areas in the country.

The Centre is within sight of Manchester Victoria Station, which is increasingly used by visitors since the opening of the new extension. Visible support for the Centre's activities from MVLR can only serve to underline the natural link between leisure facilities and the MVLR's mission to provide one of the world's best transport systems.

During last year's sponsorship, MVLR was involved in our Education Project, schools regatta and canoe expedition. Users of the Centre have often commented on this visible local support.

These three simple paragraphs take the reader straight into the rationale that sponsor and activity match. It describes the aim and vision of the charity; where the charity physically and conceptually meets the mission of the company; and how the company's previous sponsorship had generated positive comments from charity's clients.

This is all consciously a broad brush. It is no more than a brief support proposition to the image on the front cover. The aim is to provide a suitable, but swift background to the readers' appreciation of ...

Possible Benefits to Sponsor

- Full credit on advertising for Youth Afloat
- Opportunity for MVLR Management to present prizes at Youth Afloat Regatta
- Use of MVLR logo on tickets, posters, and Youth Afloat leaflet distributed across West Manchester
- Carrying of MVLR logo on Youth Afloat Exhibition and shore-based activity
- Wearing of MVLR T-shirts by staff and children attending the scheme
- Chance to offer subsidised travel to user groups
- Potential to exhibit with the Centre at other local festivals
- Recognition of MVLR's commitment to local community, in line with charitable trusts
- Photo opportunities for public affairs department activity
- Linkage to other local companies supporting the centre
- Improving the image of MVLR as a 'good neighbour' in their natural home

This page hinges on what many advertising copywriters call the transaction proposition. This is the heart of the proposal and the layout, a concise bulleted list, helps it to stand out. Often this transaction can be best envisioned as a seesaw.

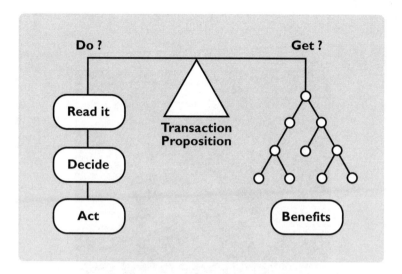

On the Do? side of the transaction proposition there are three things the reader needs to do:

1. Read it. For many these days that in itself is an unnatural act, which is why the whole thing is geared to be read swiftly and easily. Remember that the executive has many other things to read as well as this.
2. Make a decision. The layout of the proposal is geared to making that decision as easy as possible, with positive PR images, hints of natural links and good citizenship, and an extensive list of possible benefits.
3. Act on this. This is also made as simple as possible. With the second meeting already in place, the action is purely to host that meeting and agree.

The Get? side of the seesaw is mainly on this 'Possible Benefits to Sponsor' page. In advertising this is called 'benefit stacking', and demands a list of possible benefits long enough and weighty enough that it overcomes any fee objection. The reader should feel that even if some of the promised benefits don't quite work through, their money's worth is there.

Like all sales presentations it is, in part, a trick. The 'value' of the benefits which can be accurately costed are the first five: the rest offer nothing more than the warm healthy glow of the worthy donor!

What makes a good photo? Eyes, faces and action. Forget 'grip 'n' grins' (cheque handovers), architect's impressions, and beautiful but empty buildings. In this example, the sponsor is particularly keen to reach under–18s. The photo is also deliberately multi-cultural, as befits an inner city environment. The original proposal bristles with pictures of under–18s, in action, having a good time, at a specialist inner city leisure centre. It is a good idea to have a photo on each facing page.

Who Uses the Centre?

- During our 1999 Youth Afloat Scheme over 40 local groups visited the centre and over 4,000 tickets were sold
- Play schemes from all over Manchester took part in water- and land-based activities
- This year over 100 young people took part in sailing and canoeing expeditions away from the centre
- We work with many special needs groups throughout the year
- In 1998 24,500 people had sessions on the water
- A dozen local schools use the centre regularly throughout the year
- Our Education Centre works with local schools integrating National Curriculum subjects with images of life, past, present and future
- 72% of usage is by under 18s
- 70% of users live within the area served by the MVLR

In this case the company has a natural interest in the youth market. This is a key benefit to them and is therefore printed as a benefit page, showing how well the charity matches the sort of customer profile they're working on at the moment. Numbers and percentages deliberately play a prominent part, for matching with their marketing profiles.

Sponsorship Opportunity for 2001

Each year, the Centre runs an open scheme during the summer months to allow young people the chance to try all elements of watersport activity. Approximately 4,000 youngsters attended in 1999, either on the water or with the shore-based activity programme.

This scheme is in part supported by the City Council and the Charitable Foundations, but still represents a huge drain on our resources. Sponsorship would give MVLR a five-week run of activity reaching thousands of families within the area serviced by your trains.

Youth Afloat is also when the Centre is at its best – a bright and sparkling display both on the water and ashore, throughout the summer holidays.

This is a brief description of the event or project to be sponsored, with linkage to other supporters, and another reference to positive image.

Sponsorship Fee

To sponsor Youth Afloat 2001 will cost MVLR £5,000 exclusive of VAT

Sponsorship fee – How do I price this?

For many of you this is why you've brought this book. It's certainly the most commonly asked question in training courses. 'How do I price this?' Sadly there really is no simple formula that says

Costs x 2.14 = fair fee

or

We reach 8,000 people; one person = 1p; therefore the fee = £800

Go back a few steps and ask yourself what you have done. You've been to see a company; you've found out what they're interested in and how much they're willing to pay; and you've come back with a proposal based on that figure. It's your job to ensure you can afford this for the fee. It's your job to check if what you are proposing is as cost effective as other means the company could use to reach the same group. For example, consider the five main benefits in this instance:

Advertising on Youth Afloat: 12–14 PR inserts in news releases, name on two newspaper paid adverts .... @ £250 each £500

Present prizes: To support a similar event Sports Day etc. .... £500–£1,000

Printed material: Print and distribute flyers across the city .... £750–£1,000

Display of logo: Carrying of logo on exhibition and activity logo visible outside centre (similar to hoarding) .... £500–£600

Static sites: Shore based activity, seen by 10,000–12,000 people (similar to hoarding) .... £500–£600

T-shirts: T-shirt wearers – would cost perhaps £30 per day to get a T-shirt wearer around the town .... 35 days @ £30 .... £1,050
numbers wearing T-shirts balanced against repeat audience across the timescale

Sub-total £4,750
For good neighbour value and charity linkage etc. add £250

Total **£5,000**

The key is to find out how else and at what cost this advertising objective could be reached. Then you should keep your fee in that area. Do not enclose a budget, or a break down. The executive will have a fairly good 'feel' as to a reasonable fee, and after all, it was their rough figure in the first place!

This is much harder when you start out, and more difficult in theory than in practice. Effectively you're charging what the market will bear. The better known you are, or become, the larger that slice on unpriced 'profit' at the end becomes. First you must earn a reputation of delivering the promised benefit. Then you can charge for it!

NOW DECIDE:

- On a simple, practical, proposal style.
- What detail you can leave out.
- How to best display the benefit package.
- Whether you justify your fee.

---

7 **Negotiating with sponsors**

- What's the best negotiating style?
- Can't we do this by telephone?
- Is a written contract vital?
- What about inflation?

The win–win approach

Once the proposal reaches the potential sponsor, they will make the final assessment. This will be a purely business decision, based on what's on offer, from whom and what the company will get from it. They will expect to negotiate. Charity fundraisers often fail to understand how important the negotiating or 'haggling' may be to the buyer. Buyers like to feel they have actively *bought* an idea or a proposal, not been sold to. This may require, literally, a little give and take – granting a concession on one part of the package to secure the larger whole.

However – and it's a big however – business people negotiate everything. By habit and experience they know it produces the best results for them. They will believe that there's always a little more to be squeezed out of a price list or a proposal, and usually this is true. Unfair though it seems, this may be the last hurdle the fundraiser faces in convincing the executive they understand the rules of business. There are good reasons for the company to test them in this way. This fundraiser may eventually be negotiating advertising space on behalf of both events and sales packages; or be responsible for purchasing contracts with suppliers. It is not personal; it is a vital concern to the business executive that the fundraiser has the necessary skills.

The most important principle to understand is that of the win–win approach. The real goal you are aiming for after this negotiation is a relationship with the sponsor that lasts between one and three years or longer. The tone of that relationship will be set in the main by the result of this negotiation. The days in which negotiations were settled by armoured knights jousting to victory, are, mercifully, long behind us. Experience has proved, time after time, that the most successful deals are those in which both parties get as much of what they want as is possible – where both sides 'win'.

Tactics

The win-win approach means both sides working as hard as possible to meet the other's objectives. By this stage, most of the objectives for both sides should be reasonably clear. That was the key part of the fact-finding process. Two tactics stand out as particularly helpful in achieving this.

Exchange concessions

Good negotiators never grant concessions, they exchange them. This is reflected in everything they do. Their language is steeped in, 'If you … then we …' terminology; their instinctive reaction to any change sought is a counter-balancing demand; their natural rhythm is, 'Give one, get one'!

This will be tested by the executive. When you sit back down in their office or negotiating room that test will come quickly. It is good practice for you to review the stages of the proposed deal. Perhaps slip the slide binder off the proposal and take them through the proposal step by step. This is actually good negotiating practice in itself – obtaining agreements to various stages of the process. But something will probably be challenged fairly quickly, and it will often start with the price.

You have dutifully used the ballpark figure they agreed at the earlier meeting, but something has changed. The budget levels; the perceived value of the final deal; the cost of using more conventional marketing approaches could have altered since the first meeting. Don't panic. Instead, go back to the page of benefits to the sponsor; highlight two or three of the most appealing ones, such as managing directors' tickets and box, or the use of the company name in radio advertising. Then suggest that these are the items exchanged for reductions in fee. You'll probably see a smile and a nod – you've passed the first test. By offering to exchange concessions, instead of backing down and granting concessions, you have demonstrated that you will stand your ground through sound negotiation skills.

Alternatively, when they question the fee, you can also, if you wish, take them through the pricing comparisons to show how each element of the deal has been priced:

A page in a local newspaper £700

500–1,000 people see sign on building each day,
like permanent poster site £550

75,000 home leaflet drop @ 1p per leaflet £750

Newsletter sponsorship: equivalent
rates to insert in magazine with
similar circulation .... 3,000 @ £75 per '000 ..... £225

Letterhead, T-shirts, press-releases £700

Goodwill of link to charity £550

Total **£3,500**

The problem with this approach is you lay yourself open to cherrypicking – the selection of one line to challenge and debate. It's the reason we don't use budgets for sponsorship. By breaking it down you give the executive the opportunity to query each figure. They could argue that through an agency they would always expect an advertising discount of 20%, bringing £700 down to £560; if it is the same 500–1,000 people per day, that devalues the message from £550 down to £325; the leaflet is not only advertising the company, taking £750 down to £500; and so on. However, before you panic you must remember that the bulk of these figures are not real. The executive will negotiate for advantage by force of habit. Opening yourself to another tactic in the first place is falling for it, so it is best to resist the temptation to reveal your detailed figures. You are an equal in this negotiation, and you must learn to use that power.

Think strategically

The other tactic you should employ is to ponder and ask what the other side really wants. You have a primary objective which is to make a deal with a working relationship. Similarly, the executive has a primary objective or goal. A negotiating sticking point can often be sidestepped by changing focus to the other side's primary objective. Questions such as, 'What are you looking for here?' 'What's your bottom line on this point?' or 'How important is this item to you?', all help re-frame the point at issue.

● SPONSORSHIP SAGA

Everything seemed to go swimmingly until we talked about advertising the event. Then I met an inflexible resistance. The company argued that their own advertising agency must do all the advertising, and be paid their standard rates from the sponsorship fee. My fear was that the fee would be substantially used up by the agency – and on items that were actually simple posters and flyers that did not require huge creative input. After much fruitless discussion, I asked him, 'What are you really looking for here?' After a pause the answer came back, 'Safe control'. He needed to be sure that everything that carried the company's name fitted their brand image and style guide. The most straightforward way to cover himself and achieve that was by only using the creative agency that wrote the brand strategy. Once I understood his real concerns, I could work with him. We got a copy of the style guide and brand strategy to work from; the agency agreed to vet and advise on the ads rather than create and design them; their fee was an agreed, cost controlled fixed fee, of which the company agreed to pay 50% in addition to the original sponsorship fee.

The cares and concerns of all sides were addressed, the deal moved on, and achieved a successful three-year run.

In general, to achieve a win-win negotiation think carefully through the following points in the preparation and presentation of your case:
- Be fair; ask for what is fair. Win/lose negotiations or top-sided results break down far more quickly than reasoned, equitable outcomes.

- Seek exchanges. Each side must get a return for anything they offer up.
- Listen carefully to what you're asked for and do try and meet it wherever you can.
- Try and maintain as much flexibility in your position as you are able, as it encourages flexibility in the other side.
- Think strategically; think long term. For each and every item you negotiate with flexibility may bring an enduring reward once the relationship is in place.

Negotiate with confidence

Many fundraisers are beaten in the negotiation game before they enter the room. They perceive themselves as being in a weak position. In negotiation terms, the simplest definition of a weak position is one where there are few options to obtaining what you want. By the time this negotiating meeting is happening, so much time, energy and effort has been devoted to this deal that failure is unthinkable. So often we tie ourselves to a particular forthcoming event or activity whose deadline is upon us. Being driven up against a deadline is the worst negotiating position of all; the more we knock against the deadline the more concessions tumble from us, without adequate return or reward.

That is why so much of the earlier material in this book stressed the best timescales for approach; the most flexible forms of approach; and casting your net as widely as you are able. When the business suggests that you have no other place to go, they are really suggesting you should agree to a lop-sided arrangement in their favour. It is better to be able to smile and continue negotiating as if you really do have options. The best smile comes when you really do have two more companies to see next week. If you learn to do this well, the other side will never know the difference. By being confident you can create doubt about the strength of their position. If you allow the weakness of your position to show, and if you rely on their good will, you may miss out on major concessions.

For many negotiations, the difference between real and perceived strengths and weaknesses are blurred. Remember you've only got this far by playing down what the business perceives as the weakness of working with a charity, and by playing up the perceived strengths of your commercial acumen. Now you have to play that image through to the end with negotiating prowess.

Avoiding negotiation by telephone

As a fundraiser, you must beware of what may happen even before you get to the second meeting. You send the proposal to arrive on the agreed date; you have a meeting arranged for several days later. In between you're going to telephone the executive. There are two very good reasons to do this. Firstly, you must discover if they need any further information other than that contained in the proposal. They shouldn't, but it is better to have time to prepare any supplementary material they request. Secondly, it re-confirms the forthcoming appointment, and will often give you a hint as to the potential outcome.

However, by calling, you take the risk of being subjected to negotiation by telephone. Although the telephone is a common method of business communication, in negotiating terms it requires precise control of your position. With the telephone, the possibilities for misunderstandings are great as there is no visual feedback. Without body language, your tone of voice and reaction to suggestions must be carefully controlled. It is easy to get distorted messages and unintended meanings. Also, the lack of visual feedback usually makes people more reluctant to take risks by making suggestions or increasing flexibility in their position through exchange of concessions.

Perhaps most importantly, it is almost impossible to send a 'mixed message' on the telephone. You can't dilute a 'tough' proposal with a nod and a smile, or make a placating offer with a touch of impatience.

Take the earlier example of exchanging benefits for part of the fee. This can be delivered with a smile and a nod face to face – something that indicates you understand the 'testing' concept. Turning jointly to the relevant page with a smile and the words, 'Let us see which benefits we'll have to take out, then', delivers a very different message from the telephone equivalent, where the power of selecting what to drop lies blindly with you.

It is also easier to say no to someone on the telephone than it is face to face. A common point that often comes up in the negotiating phase is a request for a breakdown of the sponsorship fee. Dealt with face to face, the answer to this is two-fold. First, that the fee has been calculated based on the value of the service to the customer (the company), a figure that was discussed at your previous meeting. Second, when was the last time they discussed detailed budgets and profit lines with a customer? This last has to be delivered with a light ironic touch. Both comments effectively say 'no', but without the softening effect of personal contact the 'no' is all that will be remembered.

When you were using the telephone to make appointments you were told to keep the conversation focused on that process. The more you revealed and were willing to discuss the more likely you were to get a refusal. All of that still applies. There are very good reasons why the trust inherent in a sponsorship relationship means it is best bought face to face. One of the key face-to-face elements is this final negotiation – and any preceding phone calls must not allow this process to get off to a false start.

● SPONSORSHIP SAGA

It was brilliant! Three years with a national company, with associated brand tie-in. They were as keen as us, and the connections between our work and their image were a neat match. For us it was a lifesaver – funds that were not directly project-linked that we could use at our discretion. They were offering us £22,500 over three years; the direct cost of new items needed to deliver the sponsorship deal was around £3,400. And then they asked for a budget. Simple request. Keep the bean counters happy, you know? So I said OK.

We tried inflating the costs. Adding extra staff time. A Head Office fee. Overhead charges and fixed cost elements. We burned a lot of midnight oil on creative accounting. When we finished we knew any half-adequate accountant would drive holes through it. That's exactly what they did. They showed us how they did their pricing, and what the bottom line was for overheads etc. Their maximum was 60%. As we were a charity they'd allow us 100%. That now gave them a deal value of less than £10,000. How could we justify the extra £12,500?!?

Thoroughly miserable, I couldn't even remind them that the figure was originally theirs. A fair comparison of how they could reach a similar audience by other means. After all, the figures can't lie, can they?

The very next time our colleague above faced that problem his approach was different. On the telephone he agreed that indeed the fee was something that must be discussed at the second meeting. In his opening presentation he reminded the decision makers where the figure had come from; explained how the sum already included a discount for a three-year deal, not a single year renewable figure; suggested that like all *commercial* organisations, profit ratio per item was a confidential matter. Then he moved on, matter closed. He won the deal with the fee unchanged.

Concession tactics

We get wound up about the fee. But the majority of negotiations are settled on the non-price variables, such as the number of benefits offered; the timing of payments in relation to the sponsorship programme; and the level and method of evaluation. Remember:

- Offer your concessions a little at a time. Big concessions tend to make the other side greedier.
- Taper your concessions. As the negotiation continues, the incremental value of each concession achieved gets smaller. Or behave as if each of these tiny concessions is a loss of vital importance to you. The company will put its own values on the concessions it seeks from you, but it has no way of knowing exactly the relative importance of your concessions to you.

Faced with a demand to increase the number of free tickets to an event from 25 to 50 as part of an overall package, the likely outcome often depends on your first response. Challenge the request: What's the magic and rationale behind 50 as a number? If their list of likely attenders is higher than first thought, then make an offer, say 30 maximum, with the extra 20 tickets offered with a 10% discount on face value; then 32 + 18 at a discount; 33+ 17 is about as far as you'll go. If you taper down their expectations of large concessions, they are less likely to keep challenging you.

Some of the books and tapes you can buy on negotiating suggest keeping a big concession back for the final 'lets split the difference' moment. In a long-term relationship, allowing the suggestion that your game plan is to keep something back will merely prolong negotiation next time as they wait for you to reveal your package. It is much better to limit their expectation of achieving concessions. More importantly, if you save a big concession for the end, you invite inflexibility and a stubbornly entrenched position from the other side. If a 'split down the middle' compromise is in the air, the nearer that middle is to their side of the deal, the better the result for them. For example, imagine that the deal that is on offer is priced at £20,000, which is based on last year's successful structure plus one or two extras. Last year's price was £18,000, but the company is insisting that £15,000 will be their maximum input this year. Splitting the difference between the new and old fees is £19,000. If the company holds their extreme position at £15,000, splitting the difference produces £17,500. Being inflexible can pay well!

Timing of payments

Never be afraid to negotiate the timing of payments made by the company. You should be very precise about the amount of the fee, the length of the sponsorship, and how and when the fee will be paid. In general, the longer the sponsorship, the better for both parties. Companies that have sponsored before will know that the real benefits often don't appear until years two and three. Many are now seeking arrangements with between three and seven year horizons and beyond. However, if this a new departure for the company, they may well only want to sign for one year.

You can overcome a reluctance to commit to more than one year with a reasonable pricing strategy. If the ballpark figure you were offered for one year is £5,000, then a structured option that will bring in a two year deal for £7,500 may well swing the longer period of support. Three years for £9,500 may be even more attractive. Of course you must do your internal costings with great care, but the time and energy invested in finding new sponsors is a cost in itself which must be offset against the certainty of receiving the lower figure.

Or you could negotiate an 'option to renew' clause in the contract. If the sponsorship is successful, the original sponsor may be keen to ensure both that they continue to benefit, and that their main competitors can't come in with a better deal that rides on the original success. However, an option to renew which does not give you at least six months' leeway before the end of the contract is probably useless. Nine months to a year is commonly sought. In other words, for a three-year sponsorship, the option to renew clause will lapse at the latest by the end of year two. For a one-year deal, six months is neither a satisfactory time to measure success, nor enough time to find a new sponsor if the company does not renew. For all of these reasons, the one-year deal is the curse of sponsorship fundraising.

The amount of the fee and when it should be paid is vital information to ascertain. When talking of a three-year or longer deal, inflation clauses will be important. There are two very simple approaches to deal with this. Use the Retail Price Index (RPI) or equivalent as a guide to structure the deal to allow for inflation. For example £3,000 over three years becomes £1,000 in year one; £1,022 in year two (RPI increase 2.2%); £1,073 in year three (RPI increase 5%) – a total of £3,095. Alternatively, you could take £900 in year one; £1,000 in year two; £1,100 in year three – a total of £3,000. The first approach is probably more in your interests!

● SPONSORSHIP SAGA

When the fundraiser told us that she agreed to a bonus payment clause linked to target numbers of schools, we thought that she was mad. We had all expected cash from the sponsor as a single payment for getting the pack out to all schools. This deal only paid us for each pack used by a school, not for sending it out. Many of us felt all the risk of printing and sending the pack now rested solely with us. The schools pack sponsorship, we felt, was now dominated by the need for percentage results in a given timescale for both the pilot scheme and the national roll out. The basic fee did cover the programme cost, but any *real* earning from the scheme depended upon achieving percentage take-up results in each category of school.

To say the programme directors were reluctant is putting it politely. They refused, in the first instance, to commit to more than the basic fee would cover. But slowly, the brilliance of the concept was revealed. We recruited rapidly and widely to achieve those hated targets. Initially at our own expense, then more than covered by the bonus payments, we had a schools team with ready-made links to raise awareness and funds nationwide. The structure and investment in setting up came from the sponsor; the return, over time, was an entirely new source of income for the charity far into the future.

Sports sponsorships often contain clauses allowing for extra payments following success on the pitch, which will usually benefit the sponsors through additional media exposure. Social sponsorships find that much harder to quantify and demonstrate, although it can sometimes be done.

Be quite strict about timing of payments. Any number of statistics and newspaper articles will warn you of the difficulties of business-to-business debt collection. There is nothing more galling than watching a sponsor's name riding with yours when they haven't paid the bill. In a worst-case scenario they will look for excuses to reduce their liability after the event. You will find yourself being expected to lop the fee in response to complaint. Usually the fee is paid in annual instalments, in advance. Put in a clause that allows the charging of interest on payments 30 or more days overdue; and another that allows you to terminate the arrangement if payment is 60 or more days overdue.

Contracts – External and Internal

It is increasingly common good practice for you to have both an internal and external contract or contractual letter. For a large sponsorship, you'll probably need a formal legal contract drawn up by an established and experienced solicitor. For small local sponsorships, a letter of agreement may well suffice. There may also be some restriction clauses that the company will want to include. These may cover:

- competitive sponsors – two hoardings, two banks, double embarrassment;
- if sponsoring a publication, no advertising space sold;
- maintenance and condition of items that carry the sponsor's name – you are carrying their brand image with you on overalls and publications – faded and dirty advertising is not a positive message.

You simply need to check that none of these restrictions stop you from raising other cash or from doing an effective job for your client group. Other than that, please remember all such restrictions are negotiable. They will probably be presented as non-negotiable items, but each is a concession to a demand. Remember that you don't give concessions, you trade concessions. If your budget required both a sponsor and advertisers, then a sole sponsorship will need a higher fee. So perhaps the additional cost of image maintenance can be added to the fee? Does a hoarding sponsored by an unconnected business worry them? The second meeting gives you the opportunity to clarify all these questions and more, so it can be put in writing.

On the following pages you will find an example of an agreement drawn up between a charity and a company to formalise the sponsorship deal. It will give you an idea of what a sponsoring company may expect from you, but the specific contents must be decided in your second meeting.

The need for an internal contract is harder to understand but equally vital. One or more projects within your organisation will be carrying the weight of delivering what has been promised to the sponsor, often with an associated budget or sum of money for the project. An internal exchange of letters with the project managers setting out exactly what the team must do (e.g. wear T-shirts, put up hoardings, conduct tours for sponsor staff) can only help clarify the position. Often, charity workers will balk at some elements of the package – logos, colours, whatever. It is easier for all concerned if it is clearly written down.

In essence, this second meeting is about tying down the details. Start it with a review of progress to date, summarised in the proposal. Check the sponsoring company's understanding of and agreement to scope and purpose. Pass the negotiating tests on price and options. Debate the detail. Get it written down. Then go and deliver what you promised. Now, doesn't that sound easy?

NOW DECIDE:
- Can you achieve win-win results?
- Can you resist negotiating ploys?
- Will you be tough on payment?
- Will you contract with colleagues and sponsor?

Example of contractual letter

Fictitious Charity
16 Ford Street
Birmingham B11 2IR

Made-up Firm
99 Golden Street
Birmingham B22 3MI

1 January 2000

Dear Karen

Event: Balloon Race
Date: 14 June 2001

Please sign the enclosed copy of this letter and return it to me as confirmation that the Made-up Firm will sponsor the Balloon Race organised by the Fictitious Charity on the basis and terms set out below.

The amount of sponsorship is £15,000 plus VAT. Payment will be made against the Fictitious Charity's invoice within one month of receipt.

Fictitious will ensure that Made-up's logo will feature on all Balloon Race literature. All promotional material for the event must be signed off by the company before printing. The company will sign off publicity material within two weeks of its receipt. The logo must be printed in accordance with Made-up's house style. The Made-up staff will receive 30 complimentary tickets to the Balloon Race.

Fictitious will use its best endeavours to promote the image of Made-up and this sponsorship, although it is understood that credit in external publications and seminar handouts cannot be guaranteed.

The Made-up Firm is the major corporate sponsor of the event. Whilst the Fictitious Charity has the right to involve other companies and organisations in the event, this must be subject to consultation with Made-up, and the position of Made-up as major sponsor must not be affected.

In the event of any cancellation or postponement of the project beyond 14 July 2001 this sponsorship will be cancelled and any funds paid by the Made-up Firm will be returned immediately less any expenses properly incurred. Otherwise, the partnership outlined within will cease to exist on 31 July 2001.

The two parties will attend monthly meetings over the next 18 months to monitor progress. After the event the Fictitious Charity will submit an event evaluation report to Made-up.

The charity must treat any of the company's business as confidential and must ensure that all of its staff comply with this.

Fictitious undertakes to effect full comprehensive third party and personal accident insurance cover in respect of the Balloon Race and undertakes to indemnify and keep Made-up fully indemnified from any loss, damage, costs, or expenses caused directly or indirectly to Made-up or to any person visiting, participating or working in such event.

Yours sincerely,

Justin Mills, as authorised representative
of the Fictitious Charity

Terms and conditions agreed and accepted by:

Karen Brooks, as authorised representative
of the Made-up Firm

8 Managing the relationship

- *Who is responsible for conducting an effective relationship?*
- *Any caveats or possible conflicts?*
- *When can you talk about renewal?*
- *Will the charity's way of operating change radically?*

Project management

Conducting a sponsorship relationship is, in many ways, the same as conducting any fundraising relationship. It is built on mutual trust, respect and on contact that is frequent enough to signify the importance of the relationship, but not constantly irritating. Indeed, the fundraiser is about to become a project manager. A sponsorship relationship has all the hallmarks of a project in the ways it differs from ordinary work:

- It has a defined beginning and end, working through a sequence of agreed steps and activities.
- It uses a variety of resources (people, time, money) specifically allocated.
- It has specifications of quality and performance.
- It follows a planned, organised approach to achieve its goals.
- It involves a team of people in a joint pursuit.

As with any project, the team work better as the project moves forward. As with any project there are five basic phases:
1. Initiate an approach.
2. Plan the sale.
3. Execute the arrangement.
4. Control that process as it rolls out.
5. Prepare for the closing or ending of the arrangement in an orderly manner.

Most of this book has covered the first two phases, but now you should be ready to manage the project in phases three to five.

There are some very simple ground rules detailed below that you must get right with your approach to managing this relationship.

Commitment of the fundraiser

This arrangement has been bought and sold face to face. The fundraiser who has negotiated the deal successfully up to this point must remain as account manager, and stay in touch with the executive who bought their approach and with whichever department in the charity delivers their side of the arrangement. Charities where the sponsor is immediately handed over to the events team, or equivalent, have a far lower renewal rate of sponsorship arrangements than those where the fundraiser stays in touch.

● SPONSORSHIP SAGA

I was brought into the university to help raise funds after a number of years as a sponsorship and promotion manager with a regional sports council. The university had no track record of success with this type of fundraising. In talking to companies, I found myself increasingly drawing on my previous experience of delivering sponsorship benefits in a different, but similar environment.

One of the early successes put this quite bluntly into perspective. They wrote into their contract that I must be the account manager for the sponsorship arrangement. At first, the university hierarchy took it badly. That had not been the original idea. Once I had won the business, each department was supposed to undertake the necessary customer care for their matched sponsor.

However, the company executive insisted that this was a make-or-break point for them, and I was given overall responsibility for the project. It helped that the company congratulated the university on having the commercial acumen to appoint an experienced outsider to help them break into a new marketplace.

Commitment of the whole organisation

For sponsorship to be successful, the charity as a whole and its management must fully support both the arrangement that has been agreed and the strategy of raising funds this way. This doesn't mean the senior management of the charity has to be involved in all decisions, but it does mean that management support, adequate resources and a long-term view of success must be constant factors. Sponsorship as a fundraising strategy is about long-term gain, long-term relationships, and long-term security. Management must align its budgets and staff resources with those goals.

The charity must deliver the benefits associated with its side of the contract fairly and fully as far as it is able. In many charities, once the cheque is in the bank, a sort of sigh of relief and instant downgrading in importance of the deal takes place. The funds in place are treated as a donation to be spent, and the costs of delivering the promised benefits pared to the bone. This is a sad reflection on the short-term view that is prevalent in voluntary sector funding, and must be resisted. If the project manager has the appropriate authority in your organisation they can oversee the whole enterprise.

⬤ **SPONSORSHIP SAGA**

The problem was that I had no recognised position in the hierarchy at the university to insist that the department saw its sponsorship obligations through. The money was quickly spent on refurbishing the appropriate area, and re-equipping the library as agreed. Getting the opening event organised, the relevant plaques and acknowledgements in place, proved a nightmare. At heart, the departmental Professor felt this was not the way higher education should be funded, and it showed in the way he handled every contact with the company.

Think what you need in writing

Aside from the contractual letter itself, there are a number of elements worth getting down on paper that will help the smooth running of the relationship. Clearly this list may not be exhaustive, but will highlight some potential areas of conflict and expectation that may otherwise catch you unawares.

1. Ownership – who owns, produces, approves, has copyright to the campaign material?
2. Money – where sponsoring fundraising activity or receiving company contributions as part of a sales campaign, are there any maximum or minimum amounts, any guarantees, agreed third party auditing procedures? If you're getting 2p per item sold, what's the guaranteed minimum return? If their normal sales over six months average 2,300, then the minimum guaranteed earnings should be £46; but there may also be a maximum. If they can only produce 10,000 items over six months, the maximum expected would be £200. Some fundraisers think that for over, say, 8,000 items you should get 4p per item or a flat bonus as the deal is clearly a success. The danger here is, if you're being fair, then the deal should begin at 2,300 – as the extra items sold are the only advantage the company has. Which do you prefer? A guaranteed £46; a chance of £200, plus a renewal option if sales are raised at all; or no guarantee, a chance of £194, plus a likely renewal only if you get to the top end of the sales expectations?
3. Permission – use of name and logos. Who gives permission and necessary conditions of use?
4. Termination – under what circumstances can the arrangement end; notice periods; pay-off arrangement etc.?
5. Roles and responsibilities – who in which organisation does what?

The aim of such a discussion is to allow both sides to explore and clarify their expectations of how the sponsorship will work in practice.

Think deadlines and timescales

There is clearly a potential misunderstanding between corporate and charity cultures as to the speed of decision making. In particular, a marketing campaign, when in full swing, will often need quick decisions, to take advantage of a particular moment, or to tweak a campaign for better response. Charities tend not to be geared for fast decision making. Anticipating this by giving the fundraiser or project manager rather more devolved and flexible power of decision is appropriate. Indeed, for the charity, flexibility is often the key word. The project manager must have the authority to make and carry through decisions when needed.

Think internal PR

To manage the project effectively, take every opportunity to publicise and acknowledge the sponsorship relationship and its importance within both the charity and the company. Company newsletters will often offer a host of chances to illustrate the charity's work in more traditional ways. Companies are usually keen to highlight the good social reasons there are for supporting this cause. Well-managed sponsorship relations will often field some staff fundraising effort, perhaps some new Give as You Earn contributors and new individual covenanting members.

If the company isn't having a terrific year profits-wise, an offer to put something about this good cause element in the annual report to shareholders may be welcome. Occasionally, a charity gets the chance to address an AGM, as part of the director's reporting. Now there's a superb chance to top up the contact names in your little black book! All those non-executive directors who sit on other company's boards!

This brings us back to essential project management skills. Most would agree that the four key areas of responsibility for most project managers during the implementation phase of the project are:
1. Defining roles and responsibilities.
2. Achieving departmental cooperation.
3. Communicating effectively.
4. Being a flexible leader, which means handling problems as they come up; finding the resources to meet peaks and troughs of activity; visible and regular communication; motivating, encouraging, and enthusing the team into action.

Think renewal

A good project manager always has one eye on the end of the project. For you, the main aim for the end of this arrangement is renewal, a new sponsorship arrangement perhaps with a longer timescale. Of course the most likely renewals are from well-managed and successful arrangements already in place. Always be working on the chosen method of evaluation, keeping the figures to hand. Keep a press clipping file – blowing each story up to the size of a single A4 sheet. This soon produces a satisfyingly thick file!

Build into your meetings with the company an ongoing review of these areas: a constant drip feed of favourable background noise that creates a comforting atmosphere. The message – as in most fundraising environments – should be overwhelmingly positive. The more additional tie-ins you can create, such as newsletter articles, invitations for company directors to attend charity social events, involvement, perhaps of company pension groups with some of the charity's work, the harder it is to end the relationship.

However, the sponsorship will stand or fall by its impact on the group or groups identified in the original proposal. Throughout the project it is essential to keep a really close eye on both the original proposal and on the impact audience.

Changing society

Earlier in this book, it was recommended that you take a cold, hard look at your organisation to prepare it for the challenges of sponsorship. By now it must be very clear that the changed organisation will probably be changed forever whilst sponsorship is part of the fundraising drive. Any charity that develops the true organisation-wide commercial awareness needed to make sponsorship and the wider cause–related marketing concepts work, will never operate in the same way again. For larger charities this message is not new. They are often already market-driven businesses with a highly commercial, competitive, view of their market sector. For smaller charities this is perhaps one of the more frightening elements of the whole process. Even if short of income, the charity is often very comfortable with who they are and where they're at. In particular, they are often uncomfortable with market forces. Many of their clients are victims of market forces.

But the world around them is changing. Grants are fewer, contracts more common. Individual donors demand more involvement and better customer service. The National Lottery Charities Board demands business plans and contexts. The competition for legacies grows tougher. If charities are to grow and service their clients well they must evolve. Companies are going to turn increasingly to opportunities that give them real benefit for their community efforts. Sponsorship and cause-related marketing are the future of corporate relations. Whatever size and type of charity you are, you ignore these changes at your peril.

Standing out from the crowd

If we were talking about direct mail here, than probably we'd look at four main elements:
1. Your list – who you approach.
2. Your format – what characterises it.
3. Your timing – geared to sponsors' needs.
4. Your offer – how you can give yourself that special appeal.

In this way, a parallel can be drawn between these elements and the objectives of sponsorship. If you follow the advice in this book you will be some way toward achieving each of these aims in the sponsorship field. It is the last element, the offer – the personalisation of your charity and its activities – that is the last part of the puzzle for you to solve. You must be able to differentiate your organisation from the others in the marketplace.

Differentiation is about standing out from the crowd so that companies, customers and donors remember you. There are certain areas where this clearly can be achieved, as follows.

Attitude

This is the attitude not just of the fundraiser, but of the whole charity. Motivated, enthusiastic staff who believe not just in their cause, but in the importance of the need to fund it.

Branding

Branding about the set of beliefs, values and activities that are associated with your name. Companies guard their branded image jealously. Our differentiated image can help build theirs and vice versa.

Proud achievements

Trust and confidence can come from both the ability to adapt to changing market conditions, and a track record and history of achievement in differing market conditions. A history of 'adapt and survive' is a useful background.

Segmented messages

Tailored marketing is simply a necessity in increasingly cluttered marketplaces. More and more, all types of donor or partner are being exposed to messages tailored to age, prejudice and interests.

The advantage you have is that books like this can help prepare both you and your organisation for the challenges to come. They can help prepare you for the traps and difficulties you will face. Moreover, fundraisers who can work successfully in this marketplace will always be in demand, never short of work, and able to command the best return for both themselves and their employers or clients. It is possible that in the future, looking back, it may be the years of grant culture that will appear the oddity in the continuum of fundraising!

Go to any fundraising conference and you will find yourself rubbing shoulders with sponsorship managers from the arts, police forces, local government. The competition is tougher than ever. Companies are looking for partnership potential and an ability to raise a profile with a relevant target audience. Propose the right project, and support and cash will follow. It's not quite adapt or die, but it may be the difference between eating at the corporate table, or grubbing around in the crumbs underneath. The money and the wish to spend it is there. Go and get it.

NOW DECIDE:

- *Have you got the necessary project management skills?*
- *Can you swing the enthusiastic support of the whole charity?*
- *Do you focus on the end of the project?*
- *Is this really the marketplace for you and your charity?*

Appendix 1: sample brochures

Take our message to heart

The British Heart Foundation is fighting the UK's biggest killer through heart research, patient care and education initiatives. Please help us. Coronary heart disease is extremely costly, adding a burden of £10 billion per year to the UK economy.

Consumers are becoming ever more demanding about the companies they deal with, and linking with a good cause is a proven way to attract and retain customers. A relationship with the BHF may give you the competitive edge you need.

Corporate fundraising opportunities

- Philanthropic donations - general or earmarked
- Employee fundraising - charity of the year, payroll giving
- Sponsorship of BHF events, educational materials, campaigns
- Sales and marketing promotions
- Long-term strategic affinity cause related marketing
- Merchandising

BHF offers these benefits

- Niche appeal - 90% prompted awareness (Mori 1996)
- A range of target audiences
- Direct community links
- PR support and opportunities
- Experienced campaign team
- Network of over 400 charity shops

Still from recent BHF national television advertising campaign

Corporate partners can also benefit from BHF's network of regional offices and local branches. These links enable more focused activities, including targeted fundraising and campaigns.

Call BHF's Corporate Fundraising Team on:
tel: 020 7487 7160/9432
fax: 020 7486 3815
email: corps@bhf.org.uk
website: www.bhf.org.uk
address: 14 Fitzhardinge Street, London W1H 4DH

This extract is taken from a British Heart Foundation Corporate Fundraising Flyer: a prime example of how charities can attract company support. It is the introduction to a short flyer packed with photos and enthusiastic quotes from companies that have already worked with BHF such as Marks & Spencer and Halifax plc.

What does a partnership with Save the Children mean?

We can help you...
an association with Save the Children illustrates your company's commitment to, and understanding of, its responsibility to the local and wider community.

It creates opportunities for...

■ building bridges amongst employees, suppliers, customers, clients, stakeholders and decision makers to gain credibility, respectability and confidence in your company

■ developing skills amongst employees and business teams for increased efficiency and effectiveness

■ enhancing corporate and brand reputation and potential for increased positive publicity

■ adding value to marketing campaigns and potential for increased sales and profits

■ promoting long-term strategic interests within the local and business communities

■ networking with other companies and creating platforms for dialogue with influential bodies.

This extract is taken from *Investing in the Future*, a brochure from the Save the Children Corporate Development Department aimed at attracting company sponsorship. The brochure is packed with positive images of children from around the world and examples of how well sponsorship has worked with various international companies.

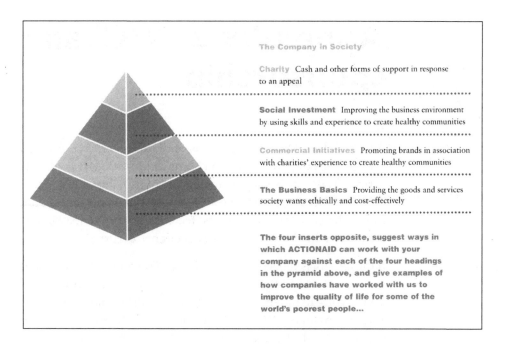

The Company in Society

Charity Cash and other forms of support in response to an appeal

Social Investment Improving the business environment by using skills and experience to create healthy communities

Commercial Initiatives Promoting brands in association with charities' experience to create healthy communities

The Business Basics Providing the goods and services society wants ethically and cost-effectively

The four inserts opposite, suggest ways in which ACTIONAID can work with your company against each of the four headings in the pyramid above, and give examples of how companies have worked with us to improve the quality of life for some of the world's poorest people...

This extract is taken from the *keeping good company* brochure from ACTIONAID. It is full of statistics, diagrams and success stories to stimulate companies into working with ACTIONAID as a professional partner.

Appendix 2: VAT and sponsorship

As far as Her Majesty's Customs and Excise are concerned, a sponsorship payment is not a charitable donation, it is taxable supply. The very basis of commercial sponsorship, the concept of mutual benefit, infers a taxable supply. The VAT office do not care if the benefits equate to the fee paid by the company, they simply need to know that some benefit has occurred.

If the charity is registered for VAT, then they must charge VAT at the current rate on their taxable supply, and issue an appropriate VAT invoice to the sponsor. The sponsor will be able to offset this VAT against the VAT they have charged to their customers on supplies made by the company. This means, assuming the sponsoring company is registered for VAT, the charging of VAT on the deal will not add to the cost of the sponsorship.

The charity must issue an invoice to the sponsor which gives both the amount of the fee, and the VAT levied; it is good practice to negotiate and agree a VAT exclusive figure prior to the issue of the invoice. In all preliminary documents always quote the relevant figures as VAT exclusive.

Smaller charities may not be registered for VAT as their taxable turnover is below the threshold required for registration, currently £50,000 p.a. If you are not registered for VAT you cannot and must not charge VAT on your sponsorship arrangements.

However, it is possible that a little success in the sponsorship marketplace, coupled with other potentially taxable supplies made by the charity, will bring your organisation above the threshold to register. You must then register, and charge VAT on your taxable supplies. For smaller organisations, the implications of the extra work involved in VAT accounting may make them ponder whether to arrange the sponsorship as part donation, part taxable supply.

This is all covered in VAT Notice 701/41 of July 1995, entitled *Sponsorship*. It can also be viewed on the Customs and Excise website at www.hmce.gov.uk

For most organisations, this situation will not apply. Generally they will already be involved either directly in VAT accounting, or indirectly through their trading arm; or will be a small organisation handling small deals all below the relevant threshold.

The VAT notice gives examples of what may be recognised as donations, and what may constitute a taxable supply. A taxable supply is not created by simple acknowledgements of support, like:
- giving of flag or sticker
- inclusion in supporters' list in programme or notice
- naming building or university chair after donor
- putting donor's name on back of seat in theatre.

However, if the sponsor's contribution is made on condition that their advertising logo is carried, promoted, or equivalent benefit, like:
- naming of event after sponsor
- display of company's logo on shirts
- display of company's logo on programme or at venue
- free or reduced price admission tickets
- access to premier or gala evenings
- entertainment or hospitality rights
- exclusive or priority booking rights.

The notice also specifically recognises that you can mix sponsorship and donations, as long as the donation is separate from the sponsorship agreement, and any benefit is not conditional upon the payment of the donation, which must be entirely voluntary and secure nothing in return. Other relevant notices are 700/1 *Should I be registered for VAT?* And 701/1 *Charities*.

Resources

Further reading

The Guide to UK Company Giving 2000
John Smyth, 3rd edition, published by Directory of Social Change,
ISBN 1 900360 68 3, £25.00

The CD-ROM Company Giving Guide 2000
Published by Directory of Social Change, ISBN 1 900360 74 8, £85 +
VAT = £99.88

Corporate Citizen
Published three times a year by Directory of Social Change, ISSN
1353-0100, £30 a year for voluntary groups

The DIY Guide to Charity Newsletters
Chris Wells, 1st edition, published by Directory of Social Change,
1996, ISBN 1 873860 11 0, £10.95

The DIY Guide to Public Relations
Moi Ali, 2nd edition, published by Directory of Social Change, 1999,
ISBN 1 900360 53 5, £12.50

Useful contacts

Arts & Business (formerly the
Association for Business
Sponsorship of the Arts)
Nutmeg House, 60 Gainsford
Street, Butlers Wharf, London
SE10 2NY
Tel: 020 7378 8143

Business in the Community
44 Baker Street, London
W1M 1DH
Tel: 020 7224 1600

Community Links
105 Barking Row, London
E16 4HQ
Tel: 020 7473 2270

Groundwork Foundation
85–87 Cornwall Street,
Birmingham B3 3BY
Tel: 0121 236 8565

Newspaper Licencing
Agency Ltd
Lonsdale Gate, Lonsdale
Gardens, Tunbridge Wells
Tel: 01892 525273